The Best
Men's Stage Monologues
of 1993

The Best
Men's Stage Monologues
of 1993

edited by Jocelyn A. Beard

The Monologue Audition Series

SK
A Smith and Kraus Book

Published by Smith and Kraus, Inc.
Newbury, Vermont
Copyright © 1993 by Smith and Kraus, Inc.
All rights reserved

COVER AND TEXT DESIGN BY JULIA HILL
Manufactured in the United States of America

First Edition: December 1993
10 9 8 7 6 5 4 3 2 1

The Monologue Audition Series ISSN 1067-134X

NOTE: These monologues are intended to be used for audition and class study; permission is not required to use the material for those purposes. However, if there is a paid performance of any of the monologues included in this book, please refer to the permissions acknowledgment pages to locate the source who can grant permission for public performance.

Contents

Introduction

Usually the director's first contact with the actor is at the audition for the production. It is ironic that at that moment when the director needs to know the most about an actor, he probably knows the least. What you are as an actor is different from what you are as a person, but revealing both is a crucial part of the auditioning process. When you choose your audition monologues, you reveal both the actor and the person. Select the best material that you can – material that will sell you as you sell it. The monologue should suit your personality and capabilities. Your choice of material reflects how you see yourself.

The selections found the *The Best Men's Stage Monologues of 1993* provide the range for a diversity of personalities and talents. I can attest to the variety of unique voices included in this volume, having produced premieres by almost a dozen of the playwrights.

An audition is designed to present what you as an actor do best. Stretching should be done in the classroom or in rehearsal, not in an audition. Choose roles within a ten-year range of your own age, depending upon your looks. This volume of monologues avoids popular and overused choices. Happily by using it, the director won't compare you with their memory of a landmark performance given by an actor whom the director has worked with in the past. Choose monologues that allow you to maintain your artistic dignity and the elements of your work that are true to yourself. Remember, you are auditioning; use what works for you. Every good monologue contains a progression from where you were before the speech began to where you are after the discoveries and decisions within your speech are realized. As you audition, ask yourself real questions and try to find real answers that require decisions in order to maintain the first-time illusion.

Remember that there is an enormous difference between acting and auditioning. In an audition, you not only imagine your partner, but you must create his or her responses and motivations as you speak. Auditions must be performed. The images you set in rehearsal for an audition must be very strong and personal to keep their effect during the nervous and artificial nature of an audition.

Relax! Concentrate first on the amount of volume you need to fill the space. Relaxing with your image of your imaginary partner can be an immense security. Trust your preparation. Economy is best! Leave the auditioners wanting more. Give your auditioners a chance to envision more than what you do at the moment. Never show your top. To do so would only minimize your work. We have all seen pinnacles of emotion before and respond better to gentle stimulation and ironic surprise.

As a person be as pleasant and warm and natural as you can. The best face you can show, especially when you introduce your material and yourself, features a smile that assures your auditioner that you are the kind of person that a director can mold and work with easily. As actor must show that, as a person, he or she is capable of humility and flexibility.

When doing a monologue for me, an actor "must have or do" the following: spirit, a connection with the material, energy from the situation, dramatic tension, a voice and body that agrees with the language, a bright mind to break the speech into smaller images, a connection with the audience, arrest the audience, and an interesting face.

This volume of unique voices and wide range of character choices will be of tremendous help in showing what you have and what you can do. As you read these monologues remember, "to thine own self be true!"

Gregory Hurst
Producing Artistic Director
George Street Playhouse

The Best
Men's Stage Monologues
of 1993

THE AFRICAN COMPANY PRESENTS
RICHARD THE THIRD
by Carlyle Brown

Papa Shakespeare, a former slave now performing Shakespeare,
50–60
New York City, 1821
Seriocomic

*All the members of Billy Brown's African Theater have been ar-
rested for performing* Richard III. *Here, the senior member of
their troupe reflects upon his character, William Catesby.*

O   O   O

PAPA SHAKESPEARE: The other night at Billy Brown's African
Theater, in the play King Richard Three, I pretend to play a
white man, name a William Catesby. And you know what
happen? The Constableman he come and take me away. They
no say what I do. Maybe they arrest me for bad actin'. They
lock me up in a cell in the Eldridge Street Jail House. Put me in
'dere with a blackbirdin' slave ship captain. Didn't give me no
bread nor water. And all that for Catesby. Tiresome little man,
that they send 'round on errands everywhere for this man
Gloucester, the King Richard Three. He's a strange man, this
man king three. He always standin' there talkin', talkin', talkin'
to hisself . . . I mean, if we was back in de islands and you see
a man there, standin' there, talkin' and talkin' to hisself. "Now
is de winter of our discontentment, made glorious summer by
dis sun a York" . . . I mean, you would say this man is crazy,
standin' over there talkin' to hisself. "And all de clouds that
lowered over de house, in de bosom of de ocean buried." You
would say, what is the matter with this man. He's sneekin'
about and rollin' his eyes, lookin' round; and ain't nobody
'dere. This the kind a thing for be madness. In the Jail House, I
had me a dream. And in my dream, I was dreaming. When all
of a sudden a great big ladder spring up from nowhere, set
right down in the middle a the room. It's standin' up, straight
up, stickin' up through the roof, way up in the sky, right on up
through the clouds. Now, I don't know where that ladder

leadin', so I wake me up. I don't want to be in dis dream. I got hard enough time being me, but I catch the devil being Catesby.

THE AFRICAN COMPANY PRESENTS RICHARD THE THIRD
by Carlyle Brown

Papa Shakespeare
New York City, 1821
Seriocomic

Here, Papa Shakespeare tells of his life in the Caribbean and of the origin of his distinctive name.

○   ○   ○

PAPA SHAKESPEARE: In the islands, where I come from, there is still slavery there. My master 'dere he call me Shakespeare so to mock me, 'cause I don't speak the way he do. He laugh. He say me brow be wrinkled so, to mark me hard for thinkin'. But I say, this man, he no wise. He no hear me thinkin' in me own way. He don't see the one he name Shakespeare. He don't see, but I remember. I remember the forest and all de rivers that come down to the lagoon. And from among the mangroves and all along the seaside, I can hear them people talkin'. And man, like my master come and take 'em away on ship and make 'em slaves. But still, I hear them. Even now, I hear them. They mouths and they tongues, they knockin' and rollin'. They go . . . (*Clucking and clicking sounds.*) I hear them. They're in my head and will stay there so long as I remember. Where I come from, the book is a living man. And we must read from what he say. It more hard for a man to lie, than a book. 'Cause we see him everyday and we know what he does and see where he goes. Everywhere them boys, they come from far. From Barbados, St. Lucia, Tortola, John's Island. From all 'round. And what they hear when they come to the towns, they must listen to the one, who can tell them the whiteman is saying. This one, who tell 'em so, he Griot. I say, Griot. Sometime, when This Man over here, wish to speak to That Man over 'dere. Each one speaks to the Griot and the Griot tells the one what the other is saying. Like so . . .

This Man say: "Griot, ask that low, snakelike dog, why is he chasing my wife."

And the Griot, he say to That Man: "That Man. This Man, he say, he knows your love for him is great, but must you love his wife so greatly as well?"

And That Man say: "Griot, tell This Man, that only a fool could love so ugly a fish face woman as his wife."

So the Griot say: "This Man. That Man he say he only loves your beautiful wife out of his great love and respect for you."

This is the way the Griot works. This what he does. If Shakespeare was a black man, he would be a Griot. So, I say, though my master mock me, it be no mock to me.

ALL FALL DOWN
by Wendy Lill

Connors, a social worker, 30–50
An office, the Present
Dramatic

Connors works with sexually abused children and here contemplates the workings of the human mind.

O   O   O

CONNORS: How do you protect yourself from the images flying around out there. How do you protect yourself from the images in your own head. A man bounces his daughter on his lap, sits on the bed and watches his wife undress, thinks about winter tires, the teller with the big hooters at the bank, how he'd like to reach out and stroke them, his daughter's musical giggles, the bruise on his wife's leg, how soft the little girl's cheeks are. He wonders if she was fifteen years older and not his daughter—but that's gone in an instant and he remembers his own mother's scent, her shining hair, sitting on her lap, feeling like the only special one in the world, and suddenly, he despises his wife, wants to strangle her, but just for an instant, maybe wants to end his own life too, all those gaping nights, weeks, years ahead, all those dark unexplored holes behind, and then that's gone too. Thoughts fly by like hummingbirds. Some of them could land you in jail but if you keep them in your head, they're harmless there—like hummingbirds. (*Ewan assembles a wooden airplane.*) I respect the mind but I'm afraid of it. There are snakes and field mice, rats and doves, lions and bunnies sleeping side by side in there. It's a miracle. It's a popping swirling miracle, and now they're all waking up together, and it scares me to death. Are we making progress here? Start at the beginning. Do the parts all fit? Is it seamless? Layer upon layer. Millions of parts. Millions of pictures in your head.

ANDY WARHOL'S SECRET GIRLFRIEND
by Richard Lay

Andy Warhol, the artist, 50s
New York City and Brooklyn
Seriocomic

In the months before his death, the pop icon contemplates the people in his life; including his secret girlfriend, Rosie.

○   ○   ○

ANDY: Well, I guess this is another fine mess I've got myself into. . . . I grew up with Laurel and Hardy but they weren't as devious as me. Why *am* I so devious? Rosie adores me and I love her, if only I could *feel* what love is all about. She puts up with all my celebrity crap . . . she tolerates my romantic shortcomings and she never complained the other night when I couldn't find my watch in the dark and tripped over her damn cat. What do I want of Rosie? Am I looking for a mate? A female mate . . . am I looking for my mother? I can't be looking for myself—I lost that person long ago. Rosie is my secret girlfriend. We met on a bus and the rest is history—except what do I do? She doesn't want to be a *secret*. She wants to go *clubbing* because she's read about what a wonderful time we all have. Ha, ha, ha. If I married her . . . if she'd have me . . . what sort of life would we have? She has this strong personality which *really* scares me. I have the celebrity . . . but a contest between her personality and my celebrity has to end in tears. . . . Then there's Gilda. I use her and she knows I do. I use her to extract her daddy's millions but she doesn't seem to care .She knows what I really am and as long as I pay homage Daddy will buy my art—my works of art which I polish off in a few minutes and which are acclaimed by the whole *ridiculous* universe. Don't try telling me it's pleasant being me. Repetition. Life is repetition, isn't it? Why do *one* painting or print when you can do a thousand which are all the same? The suckers will buy and I will be famous a thousand years after I'm dead—for doing nothing except laughing at myself. . . . Then I met Rosie. She might as well be that marble statue. She looks at me sometimes as if she hates me. Can we go clubbing? Can we go clubbing? Can we go clubbing? In the end I said yes. But there are no witnesses who can point their pointy fingers at me and say She Is Your Secret Girlfriend . . . she is my niece from the Midwest and that's that. As for Boris the Prince, he looks rather tasty, actually. . . . You can never tell with women . . . they don't have to know anything. They feel it. Intuition. No logic but lots of intuition. To be honest I don't feel too well. It's nothing you can really complain about. I feel tired but that's not unusual . . . I know, I know . . . I should get my gall bladder fixed. Gall bladder, I mean, how unfashionable. If I had AIDS we could fill Giant Stadium with a rock concert. But I don't. I just have this pain—which they will take away if go *in*. I don't want to go *in*.

ANDY WARHOL'S SECRET GIRLFRIEND
by Richard Lay

Boris, a house painter from Brooklyn, 30s
New York City and Brooklyn
Seriocomic

A convoluted course of events has landed Boris in the home of one of the world's wealthiest women. To his amazement, she has offered to pay him $1 million to paint her fabulous Manhattan apartment. Here, Boris muses on his fate, and on the woman who once broke his heart.

O   O   O

BORIS: (*Stands up and faces audience. Gilda frozen on sofa.*) I am pinching myself. I am pinching myself. This is not a dream . . . is not a dream. (*Speeds up as he goes.*) I am Boris Sullivan, I paint houses, I do an honest day's work for an honest day's pay, some of my . . . friends are wise guys and I live at home with my folks. That's the Irish side of me . . . I mistrust sincerity . . . that's the Russian side of me. I drink a lot beer and smoke fifty a day. I want nothin' in life except the knowledge that there is always a *next* house to paint. I don't want to think of myself as heartbroken . . . (*Pause and slower.*) but I *am* . . . You know, a broken heart is like the ache you get when you are in love and the ache you also get when someone you love dies . . . Rosie knew she had broken my heart . . . Oh yes, she knew. Can you break a woman's heart? I have never tried and the very thought brings tears to my eyes. . . . Oh, Rosie, why did you do it? I can't forgive you and I'm trying to forget. . . . There is an old Russian proverb . . . when a village burns down . . . another one will be built . . . (*Raises eyes and smiles.*) . . . Since I was a kid I could never express myself. Well, I'd try, but it never came out the way it should. I always did whatever people wanted of me . . . then when I was fourteen I kissed a black girl and got the shit beaten out of me by my own dad. From that moment I promised myself I would be hard and never succumb to feelings. I loved Desiree. She had a wonderful smile and we'd make up poems. They rhymed but it didn't matter . . . It didn't matter to me if she was *purple* but it did to pa. He like every color under the sun except *black*. I would have married her there and then. But I couldn't and my cop uncles took me to police bars and put me in the corner and fed me beer and let me play with their guns until I got over her.

I wanted to be a painter. My family laughed at me when I told them I wanted to be like Picasso or Matisse. They laughed at me when I said I wanted to go to art school. They laughed at me when I said I wanted to be the greatest artist in the world. So, one day my Uncle Mikhail, who was in the decorating business, gave me a big brush and some pots of paint and we went to Brighton Beach and painted. I musta painted a thousand apartments orange. That's what folks from Moscow and Leningrad wanted. . . . They were tired of red. That's when I started meeting guys from the Italian Mafia. They was young, small-time hoods but they meant a lot to me. I was lookout for a couple of times on a heist and I got given a five thousand dollar hand-out and a promise that if I ever needed any help—just give 'em a call. Ten years later I stand here and I'm offered a million dollars to do a broad's apartment. . . . Maybe the village in the proverb has just been rebuilt.

ANTIGONE IN NEW YORK
by Janusz Glowacki

Policeman, a man in blue, 30–50
Thompson Square Park, NYC
Seriocomic

Here, a member of the NYPD explains how to deal with an unruly homeless person.

○   ○   ○

POLICEMAN: Just a few years ago the communists sent a television crew over here to shoot scenes of Manhattan. So what did they do? They shot the most down and out homeless in the city. Drug addicts, alcoholics, the most unshaven raggety ones they could find and then they showed the film on Russia TV and told them they were typical New Yorkers. So anytime Reagan or Bush got on Gorbachov's back about some human rights violations, Gorby said "and what about the homeless?" Now things have changed for the better because Gorby's out. (*Earnestly.*) The homeless aren't an easy thing to deal with. There's a very delicate balance between civil rights and civil order. You know what I mean? Listen, we're in the United States, the heart of world democracy and all eyes are on us. And what is the main thing about a democracy? (*Points to people in the audience.*) Do you know? Do you? Every person has the same rights and the same responsibilities. All the regulations are the same for me, for my secretary and for you too. If the president of a big corporation comes to the park, sets a fire, lies on a bench and starts to drink liquor without a bag over it, he'll be in the same trouble any homeless bum would be in. (*Points to a very elegant, elderly lady in the audience.*) Lady, if you laid down on the floor in the Port Authority building and started smoking, the police would go to into action. We've got this all worked out. We start with phase one: phase one means we disseminate information. I come over to you and say "lady, you are violating regulations by lying on the ground and smoking. Please sit up and put out your cigarette." Now if you do that, I'll smile and say "thank you for your cooperation and have a nice day" . . . or evening, depending. And that's that, everything's copasetic. But if you, lady, say "fuck you, asshole" then I'm forced to go into phase two. Okay. Phase two, lady, means you get a warning. (*Points to a another member of the audience.*) Please. No notes. I'm telling you this in strictest confidence. You know these regulations were worked out by an expert team at the Massacheucetts Institute of Technology. MIT. (*Points to another person.*) So you, buddy. The guy next to the lady with the pearls in the sixth row. Turn off that tape recorder. Yeah, you! Not him . . . you. Thank you for your cooperation. Phase two, right? Now there's a warning. I say "Madam, if you insist on lying on the ground and smoking you will be subject to a summons." Now you have another chance to clean up your act. We're not rushing anybody. But if you answer "get lost, motherfucker" or you, lady, say "you can take that summons and shove it up your ass, you flatfooted cocksucking son of a bitch" then I am forced to move to phase three. Okay. Phase three means *steps will be taken*. Now phase three is connected with phase four, five and so on. But in phase three. Okay. Phase three requires a high level of sensitivity in the law enforcement official. The most important factor in phase three is violating your human dignity with as little force as possible. Therefore the most important moment for an officer is the proper evaluation of the would-be violator. (*Explains physically.*) In this case, you, lady. For example: do I simply handcuff you or do I twist your arms behind your back? Do I push your head down and walk you out? Do I need another officer to help me? Is a club required? Should you be dragged, pulled, pushed or escorted? Many factors enter into my decisions: are you drunk, drugged, pregnant or dead? (*Walkie-talkie squawk.*) Sorry. Gotta go. See you later.

ANTIGONE IN NEW YORK
by Janusz Glowacki

Flea, a Polish immigrant, homeless and destitute, 40–50
Thompson Square Park, NYC
Seriocomic

*Years of living on the streets of New York and alcohol abuse
have driven Flea to the edge of madness. Here, he describes his
own vision of the American Dream.*

O   O   O

FLEA: (*Holds up hands and sits back down.*) Okay. Okay. Don't get excited. (*Takes a long swig.*) You know what? You're right. You should go back to Russia where you belong because you'll never make it here. I would never leave New York myself, not for nothing. They couldn't drag me away from this place. (*Takes a sip.*) Because I know how to live in America. I read the papers. I keep up and I know exactly what to do. When I hit the bottom then I will quietly walk to one of these fancy detox centers. Look at Larry Fortensky. He's as Polish as me. He likes to have a drink and now the whole world admires him. If he didn't drink who would he be? No one would have heard of him. He would be in the construction business, painting apartments. And look what happened to him. He was drinking like a good Pole and then he slowly floated to the bottom. Maybe he had a little delirium or a little epilepsy. Anyway, he went to a very elegant detox center and who is detoxing in the next room. Elizabeth Taylor and look. From one day to the next Fortensky's lying in a hammock just rocking back and forth, birds are singing, palms are waving, Michael Jackson is dancing around, some turtles, snakes, maybe some cats. Who the fuck knows? And Liz Taylor is tiptoeing around bringing him Wibrova with grapefruit juice. Because the most important thing in life is to be yourself. (*Another long swig.*)

AVEN'U BOYS
by Frank Pugliese

Ed, a young man trapped on the violent streets of Bensonhurst
Bensonhurst, Brooklyn
Dramatic

*Driven to despair by his participation in the racial murder of a
black teenager, Ed here makes the best confession that his denial will permit.*

○   ○   ○

ED: Forgive me Father for I have sinned. It's been fifteen years
since my last confession. Look I ain't in one of these phone
booths since my dad died on the F train. Wuz gonna take me
to the Yankee game, World Series, ya know what?

He had a heart attack at Union Square. Pencils in his
hands. They thought he was asleep. They didn't try to wake
him till the train yards. . . .

The paper said it was tragic—had my glove and sand-
wiches ready. It was all set. Ain't no God I figured if I can't
even see a World Series game—waited for hours for 'im, but
Dad never showed. . . .

I got the sweats Father. Wake up with a nightmare. Everybody gets 'em I guess, maybe it's the year for 'em or somethin'. But mine got whips and stuff. Painful. I get it while I'm
foolin' around too. All I wanna do half the time is puke. I
don't get it Father. Hey, anybody call you Dad. . . .

My wife, I can't look her in the face without a knot in my
stomach. It hurts when I see her. Sometimes, she looks so sad.
. . .

She wants a kid. I think it's an excuse to screw. I look at
kids, they look weird to me, like they come from another
planet. . . .

It ain't bad to get crazy, it's just the way people is. . . .

She says you can help me. She's got a good heart. Can
you help me? Ah, what the fuck do you know. Father McGrail
used to take my hand and whip it till it bled. All you priests, always whippin' me for something. . . .

If I wuz a bigger kid, I woulda got you guys back then. You guys ever hit me again, I'll smack that collar off your neck so hard it'll take off your head. . . .

Wrong, right. Wrong, right. Wrong, right . . .

You don't know. . . .

Every hear someone's skull crack? Like a walnut. Ever watch a man, beaten, lying dead, spittin' up black blood the color of your shirt? Ever kill a man? Ever touch another man's dick? Ever think about it? Ever take off your collar and try to live around here? Just live. . . .

How many Hail Mary's, how many ten, twenty?

How 'bout a million. You think that'll help?

THE BEST OF FRIENDS
by Hugh Whitemore

George Bernard Shaw, a playwright, 60s
England, 1930s
Seriocomic

Here, the irrepressible Mr. Shaw muses on the existence of God.

○   ○   ○

GBS: We have to face the fact that we are a very poor lot. Yet we must be the best that God can as yet do else he would have done something better. I think there is a great deal in the old pious remark about our all being worms. Modern science shows that life began in a small feeble curious blind sort of way as a speck of protoplasm; that, owing to some sort of will in this, some curious driving power, always making for higher organisms gradually that little thing, constantly trying and wanting having the purpose in itself, being itself a product of that purpose has by mere force of wanting and striving to be something higher gradually, curiously, miraculously, continually evolved a series of beings each of which evolved something higher than itself. What is to be the end of this? There need be no end. There is no reason why this process should ever stop since it has proceeded so far. But it must achieve on its infinite way the production of some being, some person, if you like, who will be strong and wise, with a mind capable of comprehending the whole universe; and with powers capable of executing its entire will: in other words, an omnipotent and benevolent God.

BIG TIM AND FANNY
by Jack Gilhooley and Daniel Czitrom

Baby Creole, a black boxer and bodyguard, 20–30
New York City, 1911—the night of the fire at the Triangle Shirt-
waist Company
Dramatic

*Baby Creole volunteered to help the firemen at the horrific fire
that claimed so many young lives. Here, he tells his story.*

○   ○   ○

BABY CREOLE: I volunteered to help. There wasn't enough fire-
mens and their ladders wouldn't reach high enough. My
mother was watchin' the fire an' she said, "Luther, why're you
riskin' your life? Triangle won't even hire coloreds." But i fig-
gered iffn they did an' she was up there, I'd want someone
riskin' his life for her. I held the life nets but three bodies hit in
a row. We got lifted offa our feets an' somersaulted onta the
nets. Later, we was told that each body was like 11,000
pounds hittin'. How could we hold onta the nets when bodies
were going' right through the sidewalks? When we finally
forced open the door an' run up, I seen a guy on the second
floor. He was standin' an' lookin' outta the window. There
didn't seem to'be nothin' wrong with him. He just wasn't . . .
"there." Seems he opened the window when he smelled
smoke. An' this girl plunged past him. Whoooosh! Then annuder. An' annuder. An' then he went inta shock. Upstairs,
we come across two girls at their machines. They wasn't really
girls, though. They was skeletons . . . blackened bones.

BORN GUILTY
by *Ari Roth*
based on the book by *Peter Sichrovsky*

Rudolph, the son of a Nazi war criminal, 40s
Germany, the Present
Dramatic

Writer Peter Sichrovsky is in the process of researching a book on the children of Nazis. Here he interviews Rudolph, who details his childhood spent in exile in South America.

O   O   O

RUDOLPH: The dream is always the same. Always at night, they come, tear me out of bed, push me into a car, men in uniforms. We stop at a house. I'm shoved down stairs into a room. A white room. I'm handed a towel and a cake of soap. They rip off my pajamas. Doors lock. I look up, I see them: Shower heads. And through the holes a hiss. Hssss. Fall to the floor. Trouble breathing. Beginning to choke. Rush for the door, try to open it, bang on it, eyes are burning. Fingernails. Excrement. Silent scream . . . My parents eating cheesecake. I wake up. Soon as I close my eyes it starts again: Shower heads . . . Fingernails . . . Cheesecake.

CONVERSATIONS WITH MY FATHER
by Herb Gardner

Eddie, a Russian Jew determined to make it in America, 20–30
A tavern on Canal Street, NYC, 1936
Seriocomic

*Eddie has been made hard by life, and he here tries to impart
some tough philosophy to his infant son.*

O   O   O

EDDIE: (*Slaps the bar with his towel.*) OK, Charlie, I know what's
up, I know what you're *doin'* . . . (*Turns to stroller, smiling.*)
And I *like* it! (*Approaching stroller with diaper and towel.*)
You're *my* kid and you're not gonna say what you gotta say
till you're damn good and *ready.* So I say *this* to you—don't let
nobody push you around, and I include *myself* in that remark;
got it? Because I would be tickled pink if the first Goddamn
sentence you ever said was: "Charlie Goldberg don't take shit
from *nobody!*" (*Taking dirty diaper out of stroller.*) OK, now I
see you got a hold of your dick there. This don't bother me,
be my guest. There's many schools of thought on grabbing
your dick, pro and con. Me, I'm pro. I say, go to it, it's *your*
dick. What you hope for is that someday some kind person
out there will be as interested in it as you are. What you got a
hold of there is optimism itself, what you got there in your
hand is blind hope, which is the best kind. (*Grips edge of
stroller.*) Everybody says to me, "Hey, four bars into the toilet,
enough, forget it, Eddie—a steady job tendin' bar, Eddie,
maybe managin' a class place"—I say, "I don't work for *no*-
body, baby, this ain't no employee's personality; I sweat, but I
sweat for my *own.*" (*Deposits slug in jukebox, making a selec-
tion.*) And I ain't talking about no gin-mill, kid, I ain't talkin'
about saloons and stand-up bars—I'm talkin' about what we
got *here,* Charlie . . . I'm talkin' about America . . . (*From the
jukebox we begin to hear a full chorus and orchestra doing a
gorgeous rendition of "America, the Beautiful," all strings and
harps and lovely echoing voices.*) We give 'em America, Charlie—(*Takes in the place with a sweep of his hand as the music
fills the room.*) We give 'em a moose, we give 'em George

Washington, we give 'em the red-white-and-blue, and mostly we give 'em, bar none, the greatest American invention of the last ten years—Cocktails! (*He flips a switch, illuminating the entire bar area, the mirror glows, a long strip of bulbs running the length of the shelf at the base of the mirror lights up the row of several dozen exotically colored cocktail-mix bottles; he points at the stroller.*) OK, *Canal* Street, y'say—that's not a cocktail *clientele* out there, these are people who would suck aftershave lotion out of a wet wash-cloth— (A*dvancing on stroller as music builds.*) *Nossir*! The trick here, all ya gotta remember, is nobody's equal but everybody *wants* to be—downtown slobs lookin' for uptown class, Goddamn Greenhorns lookin' to turn Yankee—New York style American Cocktails, Charlie! We liquor up these low-life nickel-dimers just long enough to bankroll an Uptown Lounge—

[**CHORUS AND ORCHESTRA:** (*A soprano solo rising delicately as Eddie kneels next to stroller.*)

". . . Thine alabaster cities gleam,

Undimmed by human tears . . ."]

EDDIE: *Yessir*, that's where we're *goin'* you and me; I'm lookin Uptown, Madison, Lex—I got a plan, see, I'm thinkin'— (*Rising with the lush soprano.*) because there's only two ways a Jew *gets* Uptown; wanna get outa here, kid, you gotta *punch* your way out or *think* your way. You're Jewish you gotta be smarter than everybody else; or cuter or faster or funnier. Or tougher. Because basically, they want to kill you; this is true maybe thirty, thirty-five hundred years now and is not likely to change next Tuesday. It's not they don't want you in Moscow, or Kiev, or Lodz, or Jersey City: it's the *earth*, they don't want you on the earth is the problem; so the trick is to become necessary. If they need you they don't kill you. Naturally, they're gonna hate you for needing you, but that beats they don't need you and they kill you. Got it? (*His arms spread wide in conclusion.*) This, kid . . . is the whole story.

CONVERSATIONS WITH MY FATHER
by Herb Gardner

Eddie
A tavern on Canal Street, NYC, 1936
Seriocomic

When he is accused of turning his back on his Jewish heritage, Eddie offers the following bitter reply.

○   ○   ○

EDDIE: (*Turns to Zaretsky, quietly.*) Whatsa matter, you forget, pal? (*Moving slowly toward Zaretsky's table.*) Wasn't that you I seen runnin' bare-ass down Dalnitzkaya Street—a dozen Rooski Goys and a coupla Greek Orthodox with Goddamn sabers right behind, lookin' to slice somethin' Jewish off ya? Only thirty years ago, you were no kid *then*, moving pretty good considerin'. Did they catch ya, pal? What'd they slice off ya, Zaretsky? Your memory? They held my grandpa down under his favorite acacia tree and pulled his beard out—his beard, a rabbi's honor—they're tearin' it outa his face a chunk at a time, him screamin' in this garden behind his shul, they grabbed us *all* there that Saturday comin' outa morning prayers. This chubby one is whirlin' a saber over his head, faster an faster till it whistles—I know this guy, I seen him waitin' tables at the Cafe Fankoni—"I'm takin' your skullcap off," he says to my brother Heshy; one whistlin' swing, he slices it off along with the top of Heshy's skull, scalpin' him. Heshy's very proud of this yarmulkeh, he's Bar Mitzvah a month before and wears it the entire Shabes—he's got his hands on his head, the blood is runnin' though his fingers, he's already dead, he still runs around the garden like a chicken for maybe thirty seconds before he drops, hollerin' "Voo iz mine yarmulkeh? . . . Voo iz mine yarmulkeh?" The kid is more afraid of not being Jewish than not being alive. (*At Zaretsky's table, leaning toward him.*) My mother, they cut her ears off; her ears, go figure it, what was Jewish about them? Regardless, she bled to death in the garden before it got dark, ranting like a child by then, really nuts. The guy's caftan flies open, the one doin' the job on Ma, I see an Odessa police uniform underneath, this is just a regular beat-cop from Primorsky Boulevard, and the waiter too, just another person; but they were all screaming, these guys—louder than my family even—and their women too, watching, screaming, "Molodyets!," "Natchinai!," "good man," "go to it," like ladies I seen at ringside, only happier, all screaming with their men in that garden, all happy to find the bad guys. (*Sits opposite Zaretsky.*) This Cossack's holdin' me down, he's makin' me watch while they do the ear-job on Ma. "Watch, Zhid, watch! Worse to watch than to die!" He holds me, he's got my arms, it feels like I'm drowning. Since then, nobody holds me down, Zaretsky, nobody. I don't even like hugs. (*Grips Zaretsky's wrist, urgently.*) The October Pogrom, how could you forget! Livin' with us two years now, you don't even *mention* it. You wanna run around bein' Mister Jewish—that's *your* lookout— but you leave me and my kids *out* of it. (*Rises, moving briskly to bar.*) I got my own deal with God, see; Joey does a few hours a week o' Hebrew School, just enough to make the Bar Mitzvah shot—same with Charlie—I hit the shul Rosh Hashana, maybe Yom Kippur, and sometimes Fridays Gloria does the candle routine; and that's *it.* You treat God like you treat any dangerous looney—keep him calm and stay on his good side. Meanwhile . . . (*Takes folded legal document from cash register, smiling, proudly.*) Today, today the Jew lid comes off my boys. (*Striding back to Zaretsky's table, opening document with a flourish.*) Check it out, Anton, you're the first to know—(*Reads from document.*) "Southern District Court, State of New York, the Honorable Arthur Gladstone, presiding. Application approved, this Third day of July, of the year Nineteen Hundred and Thirty-Six; Change of Family Name—" (*Holding document aloft.*) Yessir; so long, Goldberg; as of one p.m. yesterday you been livin' here with the *Ross* family—outside, take note, the sign says "Eddie Ross's Golden Door"; shit, I just say it out *loud,* I get a shiver. (*Sits next to Zaretsky, pointing to photos over bar.*) "Ross," yessir—honor o' Barney, "One-Punch," Ross and Mr. Franklin Delano Roosevelt, friend of the Jews, God bless 'im. (*Leans toward Zaretsky.*) Goldberg sat down with ya, pal . . . (*Slaps table, stands up.*) but Ross rises. (*Striding briskly up toward bar.*) And he's got business to do!

THE DESTINY OF ME
by Larry Kramer

Ned Weeks, an AIDS activist who has volunteered to participate in an experimental treatment program, 40s
Autumn, 1992, just outside Washington, DC
Dramatic

After many frustrating years of battling social ignorance, political treachery, and disease, Ned allows himself to become a human guinea pig for the very establishment he despises. Here, he vents his anger and despair.

O   O   O

NED: (*Changing from his street clothes.*) What do you do when you're dying from a disease you need not be dying from? What do you do when the only system set up to save you is a pile of shit run by idiots and quacks? What do you do when your own people won't unite and fight together to save their own lives? What do you do when you've tried every tactic you can think of to fight back and none of them has worked and you are now not only completely destitute of new ideas but suddenly more frightened than you've been before that your days are finally and at last more numbered and finite and that obit in *The New York Times* is shortly to be yours? Why, you talk yourself into believing the quack is a genius (*Massages his sore ass.*) and his latest vat of voodoo is a major scientific breakthrough. And you check yourself in. So, here I am.

A DISTANCE FROM CALCUTTA
by P. J. Barry

Buddy, a man with a learning handicap, 25
A home in Jericho, Rhode Island, 1923
Dramatic

Buddy is a simple man who has taken a room in the home of his employer's mother. He soon falls in love with Maggie, his boss's outspoken sister. Here, he tells her of his painful childhood.

O   O   O

BUDDY: My father made everybody call me Buddy. He wanted nobody calling me Edward Junior because I wasn't like him, oh, no. But I was good in geography . . . you know . . . even when I was ten. I'd already been held back, but one day I came home from school and I recited all the states to my mother. She was proud of me, said so, made me say them in front of my father when he got home . . . sitting there in his chair with the newspaper . . . and when I finished my mother clapped and Buster barked and my father said: "Fine, but what about arithmetic. What's ten times ten?" I said twenty and he got all red in the face and got up and whacked me with the newspaper this time over and over until he made me cry in front of him and that's when I bit him on his hand and I *held on* with my teeth and Buster bit his other hand. Did my father yell! Did my mother scream! She got me loose and they got Buster outside, and I never saw Buster again, they had him drowned. They came back into the house and they found me, I was hiding in the cellar holding onto the banister, and my mother screamed: "Look what you've done to your father, you're not only stupid, you're crazy, too!" and my father took off his belt and even with his hands all bloody he beat me and beat me and I got bloody and my mother got scared and called her sister, my Aunt Tish, the nurse, and my Aunt Tish came and said if she had a gun she'd shoot both of them. She took me to her house and gave me a bath and put salve on my wounds and bandaged me and hugged me . . . and a week later she took me home and said if they ever laid a hand

on me again she'd go to the police. They didn't touch me.
They sent me to the Sisters of Mercy in Pawtucket.

DISTANT FIRES
by Kevin Heelan

Foos, an African-American construction worker, 30s
The tenth floor of a construction site, Maryland
Dramatic

When Foos is accused of being involved in the race riots that are plaguing the community, he tells a bitter tale of a walk he took on a hot summer night.

○   ○   ○

FOOS: I didn't do nothin' man. 'Cept walk outta my house and up the street. Like I always do. I pick up some ice cream like I do when the heat in my house gets so mean I wanna swing at it. Takin' that walk and stickin' that cool ice cream in my throat is the top part a my night. 'Tween passin' out and suckin' on 'at cream ain't nothin' but Cambridge. I'm walkin' back and I hear a police say "There he is . . . there the muthfucker," and it's lights in my face so fas' my heart can't keep up wid me and 'm the coon stuck in the road, the truck comin' ninety miles an hour and then shit—Jesus God—my side, my ribs. I'm fuckin' dead and the dirt and ants and sand and a ridged heel on the back a my burnin' neck. A police standin' over me . . . "That's him. That him? No. Yes. . . ." . . . me . . . me . . . no . . . no, no . . . I'm Foos, man. I ain't Harris. I ain't Harris. I'm Foos. *Please!* And then up into the lights. No face on the cocksucker . . . just "Zat him? Izat him?" Then my nigger picture on a card from my wallet and the down voices. No face, just sad voice sayin', "No. Fuck. That ain't him. Just a nigger eatin' ice cream." So my walk comes back to me and I say, from some-place I don't know 'cause I'm so jacked, I say, "Gimme back my fuckin' ice cream." To backs I say that. . . . One second a pure balls and their fuckin' backs is all that hear. And I pick up my ice cream 'cause goddamn if it ain't the one thing I look forward to in my Cambridge life . . . and I eat the crunchin' sand and the dirt with oil . . . and I eat maybe even a sliver a glass and I hear my brain talkin' . . . "Fuck 'em up, Foos. Skin 'em up, Foos." But while I listen to my brain, somewheres else is picturin' the glass rippin' my insides to shit and back and that somewheres else tells me to keep on eatin'. And I walk like I always do and eat the cream and don't spit out the glass may be there. Fuck 'em up, Foos. Eat the glass and lay down Foos. Split like melon. For one walk on one Cambridge night. I did nothin'!!

DOG LOGIC
by Thomas Strelich

Hertel, a man suffering from slight brain damage after being
shot in the head by his father, 30–40
An old pet cemetery in a remote area of California's Central Val-
ley, the Present
Seriocomic

*Hertel is far more in tune with his need to survive than are most
people. When he senses that his wealthy mother is about to
make a deal with a powerful real estate company to sell his land,
he is reminded that life feeds on itself.*

O   O   O

HERTEL: (*Addressing the dead pets.*) You smell it? (*Smells the air.*)
You recognize it? You know that smell, you know what she's
gonna do. Unmistakable. Goes way back. Before we were
pets, before we were domesticated even, back when we were
all still wild. Before we lived in trees and houses, we lived in
burrows, caves, dens. Packs of us keeping each other warm,
breathing each other's air, the feel of the earth, cool, safe,
holding us close, protecting us. (*He pikcs up a shovel.*) It can't
anymore. Not in the current business climate. You know, you
been there. Hiding in a hole, silent, trying not to breathe in
the smell of something bigger than you, knowing it's out
there, waiting—the claws, the teeth. They don't give a shit.
Can't reason with 'em. Only one thing to do (*Beat.*) They mark
us you know, teeth. Identify us, uniquely. They dig up a pair a
million year old molars in the Olduvai gorge, and calculate that
the guy was five feet tall, ate a high-fiber diet, and that his favorite color was blue. Or some hunter finds a pile a bones and
rags in a gully—who is it? Look at the teeth. What's left after
everything else is dust? Teeth. All kinds, (*Urgently.*) man-teeth,
dog-teeth, amoeba-teeth—them too, it's the concept. Teeth
that can chew through anything, skin, muscle, bone, trust,
love, souls. The hard little pieces of us that can survive anything, fire, time—everything but neglect. The hard little pieces
of us we use to tear life apart, consume it, survive. We're none

of us innocent, it's something we all got in common, as animals. Life feeds on itself, now, then, forever. (*To the animals. Anita stands silent, motionless, watching him.*) It's not a moral issue, not in the traditional sense, you do what you gotta do that's all. To survive. I hope you'll understand. Why I have to do this. Don't judge me.

DOMESTIC VIOLENCE
by Frederick Stroppel

Michael, a man on the verge of ending his marriage, 40s
A bedroom, the Present
Seriocomic

Michael can no longer tolerate his wife's constant quest for perfection and here tells her of his malcontentment.

O   O   O

MICHAEL: How much happiness can a man take? I've had my fill! I'm fed up!

[**SANDY:** I don't understand . . .]

MICHAEL: For Christ's sake, we've been married ten years and for ten years you've been the perfect wife. You never complain, you never demand . . . you completely subordinate your own wants and needs for the sake of my casual comfort. I lift a finger, and you jump. I get drunk, you tuck me in bed. I gamble away my paycheck, you console me. I take off a dirty shirt, it's clean by morning. I go to work, there are flowers on my desk. I go to the bathroom, there's full roll of toilet paper. A full roll! Every time! How do you do that? Any other woman would castrate her husband if he went to a football game on their anniversary. Not you. You buy me tickets! How do you think that makes me feel?

[**SANDY:** Happy?]

MICHAEL: No! Not happy! Sick! I'm sick of it! I can't take this shit anymore! Did it ever occur to you that maybe I don't want a perfect wife? That maybe I'm tired of seeing you do everything right? That maybe just once I'd like to see you make a fool of yourself? Or say something vicious? Or do something *human*? In ten years of marriage, I don't think I've ever heard you fart. I don't think you can.

DOWN THE SHORE
by *Tom Donaghy*

MJ, a drifter, late 20s
On the street next to a church outside Philadelphia, the Present
Seriocomic

MJ has returned home to suburban Philly after several years of drifting from one job to another. When he encounters his 15-year-old sister, he is shocked to discover that she barely remembers him. Here he tries to jog her memory with a story of a long-forgotten family vacation to the sea shore.

O   O   O

MJ: We, uh, we went down the shore. Together a few times. I know you don't remember this. You were a really little kid. We went down. You, me, Sal Sal. Stan Man.
[**LUKE:** Down Avalon?]

MJ: Avalon, yeah. Went to Sea Isle summers after that, before that Avalon. Never Ocean City.
[**LUKE:** Ocean Shitty.]

MJ: Right? So, but we were playing cards one night. You, me, and Sal Sal. Stan Man off somewhere. But you weren't playing, just pretending, looking at the rain. Seemed real peaceful. Looking at the rain. Three of us quiet. Quiet that comes in down the shore when the rain comes in. Sunday rain comes in. Sun's gone in. Rain kept coming. Kept playing cards. Then really coming. Sheets moving, moving walls of rain. Kept coming. Put my cards down. Walked out to the patio balcony—we had the second floor—water's up to my feet.
[**LUKE:** Up that high?]

MJ: [That high up.] And we'd some Boone's Farm, so didn't seem weird or nothing that all the houses were missing their first floors. And I'm getting drenched. Then this rowboat floats by. Nobody's tied it down, guess. I stop it. Look in at your little face. Sal Sal passed out on the table. You toddle out to the balcony. I pick you up, put you in, then me. Paddle with my hands down the river in the street. Paddle past all the roofs paddle till the rain stops. We just float.

[**LUKE:** Did?]

MJ: [Yeah.] Then sun sneaks out little. Just little, then purples, seeping. Blue seeping. Everything more quiet even. You hold my hand. Your little hand. And we danced, in the boat, 'cause kinda scared, but kinda not caring on account of it's all so unreal. Can't take it serious, don't recognize anything. Little dance, so we won't tip it. Then you go, "The world is drowning. Has anyone told Jesus the world is drowning?" Told you the world's just taking a bath, said, not drowning. But said I'd call Jesus, just in case, tell him just to make sure. And he could do CPR. Just in case. Mouth to mouth, on the world.

[**LUKE:** That happened?]

MJ: [Yeah.] Later, you told Sal Sal Jesus gave the world mouth to mouth and I got slapped 'cause she thought I was feeding you some perverse shit.

DREAM OF THE RED SPIDER
by Ronald Ribman

Uttyersprot, a rag picker turned political informant, 40–50
A country enduring a military dictatorship
Dramatic

Uttyersprot, a henchman for a corrupt regime, has led a good and honest man to his doom. As he watches his victim bleed to death, he tells him of the inner torment that has driven him to his present state of being.

○   ○   ○

UTTYERSPROT: These are the pictures I was taking of my wife before she was struck down by that joke that came out of nowhere. You see that shadow? An open field, no bush, no tree, no clouds—so what is making that shadow? Not me! (*Shuffling pictures, one after the other, under Don Emilio's eyes.*) You see how as I move around taking pictures my shadow moves around because of the sun? But this shadow doesn't. It doesn't move in the sun because it is not a shadow cast by the sun. It is from something we can't see, something that makes a shadow across these pictures like a cold nightmare. Do you know what you are looking at, Don Emilio? You are looking at the presence of God on earth! (*Throwing up hands as one would if he encountered a madman saying mad things.*) How could this be? The man is mad! God casts no shadow! But I tell you it is possible. What am I to the microbe on the floor in front of me? Nothing. A shadow cast down from a dimension it cannot even be aware of. And that is what God is to us—a shadow from a place we cannot even begin to conceive for all our cunning. And that is what I am looking for, Don Emilio—the shadow that shouldn't be there; the shadowed presence of God drawn into this room like a tiger drawn to the bait of a tethered goat!

THE GAMBLERS
by Val Smith

Hayes, a reverend by turns ominous, erudite, devilish, and kind,
40s
A sidewheeler making its return down the Mississippi from St.
Louis to New Orleans, just before the Civil War
Dramatic

*Hayes has traveled the Mississippi as a gambler for many years.
Loneliness has taken its toll as he here reveals to a fellow traveler.*

O   O   O

HAYES: Well. I do not presume to know how it is with those of
the gentler sex, Mrs. O'Bannon. But, for myself, I'm no
stranger to loneliness either. Or longing. Such feelings are
powerful.

[**MRS. O'BANNON:** Truly.]

HAYES: Why, there have been nights, more than I care to number, when I have been laying there—in the darkness—can't
sleep—nobody about—nothing at all to do.

You start thinking, you know, about things. There in the
dark. All the getting and doing which only a few hours before
seemed so important—necessary—and all of it suddenly loses
its meaning. All of it. Days and nights, they just blend together
so you can't distinguish one from another. You try to pick 'em
out but you can't. So you're left with this—gray ribbon
stretching all the way back as long as you can remember. And
forward, too, further than you want to imagine. Endless. All
the way to the grave.

And there it is. A dull, gray, ordinary thing. Your life.

And so to save yourself, you recall the brighter moments
you stored away. Silly mostly.

A small fine hand on the railing. A ringlet that's come
loose in the breeze, glinting in the sun. The murmur of a
sweet voice through the wall. Scent of lavendar water. The
rustle silk makes going by. Sometimes it's a face you once
tipped your hat to, admired in passing, and thought no more

about. Until right then.

Those moments sustain you. And pain you like fire. But they're all you have and somehow, they get you through. Through all the might-have-beens and should-haves-and-didn'ts. All the regrets you now own because it's always been more important to watch the table. And keep your eye on the god almighty cards in your hand.

GLENN
by David Young

The Puritan, an aspect of Glenn Gould's personality, 30–40
Inside the imagination of musician Glenn Gould
Dramatic

Keyboard player Glenn Gould was a complex genius. Here, the puritanical aspect of his mind discusses performing, art and morality.

O   O   O

PURITAN: (*Reading from his pad.*) Catharsis, from the Greek *catharein*, meaning "cleanse." The warrior must be cleansed in battle. Before taking the field he must temper his sword with all that he knows, anneal the blade in the fires of his deepest beliefs. (*The Puritan picks up his writing pad and moves toward the piano, reading from the pad. He speaks with great gentleness, an inward quality.*)

I believe a musical performance is not a contest but a love affair and that love affairs must be conducted in private. I believe that public performance is the last blood sport and that applause is a shallow externalized expression of brute herd instinct: the howling mob is composed of passive individuals and passivity is the enemy of art. (*With growing conviction.*) I believe that everything that is involved with virtuosity and exhibitionism on the platform is outward looking, or causes outward lookingness, and that that is sinful, to use an old-fashioned word. I believe that the purpose of art is the active lifelong construction of a state of wonder and serenity. (*He moves past the other players one by one, addressing them individually. The performer is first.*)

Morality has never been on the side of the carnivore. Evolution is the biological rejection of inadequate moral systems. (*He turns his attention to The Perfectionist.*) Our evolution in response to technology has been anti-carnivorous to the extent that, step by step, it has enabled us to operate at increasing distance from our animal responses. Technology imposes upon art a notion of morality which redefines the idea of art itself. (*He pauses, thinking.*) The deep question is: *Why* do I believe as I do? Because my beliefs are true . . . or because I need them for reasons that are forever lost in the rear-view mirror? The emotional line runs deeper still . . . the warrior must see himself in a new light . . . he must learn to *listen*. . . .

I HAD A JOB I LIKED. ONCE.
by Guy Vanderhaeghe

Les, a boy accused of indecent assault, 18
A police station in Saskatchewan, 1967
Dramatic

Les maintains the swimming pool at the local club. During his interrogation at the police station, he tells the sergeant that he feels isolated from the other kids.

○   ○   ○

LES: It only came to me this summer, you know? That I was invisible. (*Laughs.*) I mean, fuck, I thought I was flesh and blood and solid but certain people, certain *kinds* of people, were looking right through me. Not all people, like my old man sure as hell sees me because who else is he fucking yelling at? And Mike, he sees me, and the girls who have to work at the Dog 'N Suds, and the old ladies who shop at the Saan Store—these kind of people can see me. But the other kind—the ones that live in the nice houses, the ones that drive the Chrysler New Yorkers and Buick LeSabres, you know, the ones who sit on the Recreation Board, the fat old farts who waddle around the golf course and tip you a fucking dime for hauling their golf bags around after them for three-and-a-half hours when you're thirteen years old, and blame you because they hit a duck hook, you were supposed to've moved or something— they look right through you, to them you're invisible. (*Pause.*) And their kids too. To their kids you're invisible. (*Pause.*) Like Tracy and her crowd at the pool. I stood right up to the grill but they never saw me. Didn't have a clue I was there. (*Pause.*) I studied them. Jesus, I even knew whose beach towel was whose. I spot an empty beach towel and I knew who'd jumped in the pool. The girls—they never swim—they just jump in when they get too hot from tanning. And the transistors going all the time, full blast. When the pumps are shut down I hear the music. Afternoons they always listen to Regina because during the day reception from Winnipeg is not so hot, but if they come back to the pool at night, they play Winnipeg because you can pick it up better at night and they got lots better disc jockeys on Winnipeg. (*Pause.*) Nights they had parties. Teen parties, I mean. Somebody would bring a barbecue to do hamburgers and hot dogs. And there'd be a portable record player for dancing. (*Speaking quickly.*) All the floodlights shining down and the underwater lights in the pool turning the water a beautiful green and the sky pitch black, or sometimes a big yellow moon, and everybody dancing in their bathing suits. (*Beat.*) I used to sit in the dark and watch them. Soon as the party started I'd turn the lights out in the pump room. If I'd have had a light on they could have seen me watching at the window, right? So I sat in the dark. I held my cigarette like this. (*He holds up a cupped hand.*) So they couldn't see the tip burning red in the window. My old man said that's the way they did it in the war, so they didn't give themselves away to the enemy. (*Beat.*) They didn't even know I existed.

THE ICE FISHING PLAY
by Kevin Kling

Junior, a fisherman and bait shop owner, 40s
An ice fishing house on a lake in northern Minnesota
Seriocomic

A man of simple taste, Junior here reveals his dislike for artists.

O   O   O

JUNIOR: You know, me and Cookie are trying out a new restaurant in town if you wanna go.

[**RON:** No, thanks, though.]

JUNIOR: We've been doing that. Went to one the other day "Peace Meal" it's called. I look on the menu, where's the four basic meat groups? And then you gotta ask for white bread. I got a plate of one of the terrible T's I can't remember tofu tamari tahini tabouli something. Washed it down with the swallows of cappacino and look, I got nothing against vegetarians, some of my favorite foodstuffs are vegetarians, but I left hungrier than when I walked in, cut my mouth on my coffee cup that had a sculpture of an endangered species on the rim of the mug, sea urchin got me. Made me hope the damn things do go extinct so they don't put 'em on the coffee mugs. No offense to Irene but the artists ruined everything.

[**RON:** You can't say that, Junior.]

JUNIOR: Use to be there was no such thing as art. If there was a drawing it was to say how to kill something . . . or a song was to bring rain, people used to know why they beat drums, now you get these nincompoops coming up from the cities with a new shirt and a twenty dollar bill and they don't change either, beat some drums in the woods for a week, don't even know why, go home have sex with their wives till they forget how, and have to wait another year to come up here again. And it was the goddamn artists come up here and turned us all into metaphors, once you're a metaphor you can't do nothing without it meaning something. I got to hand it to Irene, though, she seen it coming. Was smarter than the rest of us.

[**RON:** I think she just liked to paint, Junior.]

JUNIOR: She turned your perfectly good resort into a artist colony.

THE INTERVIEW
by Amy Hersh

Colin Bradshaw, an English actor, 40s
London, 4 years ago
Seriocomic

When a pretty young reporter from the Washington Post interviews this well-known Shakespearian actor, he breaks his own rule and speaks of his divorce.

O   O   O

COLIN: What a fiasco "Henry" was. The unhappiest time of my life, between the show, and the divorce.
[**INTERVEIWER:** I've been instructed not to talk to you about that.]
COLIN: No, it's all right. It's about time. It was all over the tabloids, anyway, and neither of us said anything publicly. Only thing Jane and I ever agreed on. I'm ready to talk about it.
[**INTERVEIWER:** Are you sure?]
COLIN: [Yeah.] See, when I got into "Henry," my marriage was almost over, and I was still in love. There was nothing to do but stay drunk. It was over. So, I tried to stay drunk every possible minute I wasn't on stage or rehearsing. I never once was drunk during a performance—I'm very proud of that. But somehow (*He laughs.*) I thought nobody would notice what was happening to me. I thought it was all invisible. I also thought the 30 pounds I'd put on was invisible to everyone. Madness.
[**INTERVEIWER:** Did you have any friends who talked to you about it, or said anything?]
COLIN: [I don't have friends like that. I've got an agent and a manager. Not the same.] I guess my friends were too scared to tell me. So anyway. Arrogance, really. "Oh, I'm such a great actor, I'll fool everyone." You see, I'm still learning about my craft. The whole point about acting is: You're not fooling anyone. And every single review had the same line: "His Henry

was a disappointment, but he certainly is a bloat king."

Oh Christ. And every time I opened my mouth to say "Where is my gracious Lord of Canterbury?" all I could think was "The Bloat King." You imposter. And now they've found you out.

"Despite a valiant attempt by Colin Bradshaw, his Henry lumbers about the stage, draped in nondescript medieval rags apparently designed to hide a good deal of excess weight." *The Times.*

"Watching Colin Bradshaw's Henry is like watching the world through dark gauze: nothing is ever in focus, and everything begins to look the same after a few minutes. An honest evaluation can't be rendered without mentioning how frankly shocking it is to see Bradshaw's pronounced weight gain. Perhaps the actor has reached his peak and is now in sad decline." *The Sunday Times.*

"He was cast as Henry V because his name is Colin Bradshaw. More appropriately, he should have played Falstaff." *The Manchester Guardian.*

Variety's review was the best. "Bradshaw's Hank Sank." (*He laughs for a moment.*)

It was devastating. Worse than the divorce. So I dropped out of the play, rented a house in Barbados for four months. And I ran on the beach every day, and stayed on a liquid protein diet. Lost 30 pounds, plus. It was a turning point in my career.

See, I never drank before that, so I don't consider myself an alcoholic. It was something available to abuse myself with, but it wasn't anything personal, if you see what I meant. I could have wrecked my car, or gotten an ulcer. Alcohol was simpler. It was so funny, when I got back. Someone said to me, "Oh did you do the 12 Steps?" I didn't even know what that was. I thought it was some kind of exercise. So I said, "No I didn't do the 12 Steps, but I did a good deal of swimming."

Here I am now, 30 pounds thinner. I've gotten all that self-destructiveness out of my system. And I think I'm a much better actor. I'm very proud of it all.

(*Leaning into the mike.*) Did I mention that I lost 30 pounds?

INVENTING AMERICA
by Jeanne Murray Walker

Frederick, a Russian farmer, 38
A poor farm in the Ukraine, summer 1909
Dramatic

To avoid military service in the upcoming war, against the wishes of his pregnant upper class wife, Frederick has decided to move his family to America.

○   ○   ○

FREDERICK: *Who will I be in America?* you cry. You'll be my wife! Didn't I go straight from the arms of war to a marriage broker? I threw down a ruble and studied his shoe box full of photos. Yours had eyes like my father, eyes like coachlights bobbing way, dreaming. But not of me—of store-bought soap, of circuses and oranges. How can I buy such things in this country? For months I've told you, *we can't stay here!* But you and your sister lie in our dark parlor trembling like the rabbits I killed last night for dinner. You test my patience. In heaven God will ask me, not you, what I've done with the talents he's given us. You've had five children quick as nails pounded in a board, and another bulging out—a boy, by the way you're jutting–like me, to be snatched from his bed for war. But what do you know about conscription? The Cossacks riding up, guns hammering on doors, and Russia's promises to us Germans as rotten as old wood. They battered my mother, poured in, and found me so I could kill the Japanese for them. Now Russia holds this gun against my head: they'll take my son to fight their wars. Against them, I am one man who speaks one language, able to die once. But in America we can make many choices. In a book I saw Minnesota, a circus of bright flowers: Queen Anne's lace, snapdragon, verbena, forget-me-not. I knew you would love them all. So yesterday I crept into our bedroom and pulled your dowry from the secret pocket of your nightgown. I've already spent it for our passage. Your sister's husband has done the same. But his voice has left him, and I have to stand here for us both. (*Pause.*)

Why should you cry? I'm a soldier again, alone, walking into a snowy field to face you, more frightening than an enemy whose words I can't understand, whose guns are aimed at me.

ISABELLA DREAMS THE NEW WORLD
by Lenora Champagne

Ferdinand, a young man seeking a new life in the city, 20s
Louisiana, the Present
Dramatic

*His father is a Ku Klux Klansman and his mother lives in a world
of dreams and visions. To escape, Ferdinand travels to the city
where he plays his horn on the street.*

         O   O   O

FERDINAND: I'm sick of them all. Sick of my out-of-it mother, who named me after a bull who wouldn't fight. Sick of the hatred that is my father, the famous white supremacist. Sick of my bossy grandmother, sick of the South and the trees and the dirt and the smells and always eating rice. This pond is too small. (*He picks up his toy truck.*)

My red truck waits beneath the banana tree. Time for the getaway. The Harley boots are stashed under the seat, the maps to new places stacked on the dashboard. Let's burn some rubber. (*Throws the truck off.*)

I wipe my big hands, coated with car grease, on my oil rag. Twenty tires in one day is too many changes. My corner of the shop is a hot box; I sweated through my first shirt and the spare one. Soon all this will be history, stories for the new people I'll meet—if I choose to tell. I'll go somewhere as a stranger and start my life.

I take a shower and shave carefully. I slick my hair back. I put on clean jeans and a fresh shirt. This will be the last time I look at myself in this harsh light.

I head north in my truck. Riding along that highway, the engine purring beside me, I finally feel what freedom is.

(*The big city. Music and lights change. A woman walks across, a man approaches her, "Smoke, smoke." A girl dances across with a Walkman; a black boy watches a bag lady.*) I enjoy being a wild thing in the city. Girls here are pretty and they like to hear me sing. I play my horn for money and I do as I please.

I move around; I don't stay still. I see lots of new things and sleep where I can. When I get jittery, I go to the pier and jump around till I calm down. I like the smell of the river, and the separation from the other side.

You can walk all day without saying a word.

[**VOICES**: Smoke, smoke. Hey, daddy!]

FERDINAND: When people talk to me, I talk back. If they want something I keep moving. When I have something extra, I give it away. The way to live here is light and free. (*A man steals his horn.*)

Hey! Give me back my horn! (*He runs off. He comes back on.*) People stop listening when I sing, so I help the Koreans for peaches and beans. (*Picks up a crate.*) People throw away such good stuff! I can use this. I sit under trees and watch pigeons in the park. When the weather changes, I stick some feathers in my hair for confidence. Now I'm a wild Indian in the city.

JEFFREY
by Paul Rudnick

Jeffrey, a gay man determined to give up sex, 20–30
NYC, the Present
Seriocomic

Here, Jeffrey bravely renounces sex.

O   O   O

JEFFREY: Okay. Confession time. You know those articles, the ones all those right wingers use? The ones that talk about gay men who've had over 5000 sexual partners? Well, compared to me, they're shut-ins. Wallflowers. But I'm not promiscuous. That is such an ugly word. I'm cheap. I *love* sex. I don't know how else to say it. I always have, I always thought that sex was the reason to grow up. I couldn't wait! I didn't! I mean—sex! It's just one of the truly great ideas. I mean, the fact that our bodies have this built-in capacity for joy—it just makes me love God. Yes!

But I want to be politically correct about this. I know it's wrong to say that all gay men are obsessed with sex. Because that's not true. All *human beings* are obsessed with sex. All gay men are obsessed with opera. And it's not the same thing. Because you can have good sex.

Except—what's going on? I mean, you saw. Things are just—not what they should be. Sex is too sacred to be treated this way. Sex wasn't meant to be safe, or negotiated, or fatal. But you know what really did it? This guy. I'm in bed with him, and he starts crying. And he says, "I'm sorry, it's just—this used to be so much fun."

So. Enough. Facts of life. No more sex. Not for me. Done!

And you know what? It's going to be fine. Because I am a naturally cheerful person. And I will find a substitute for sex. Sex lite. Sex helper. I Can't Believe It's Not Sex. I will find a great new way to live, and a way to be happy. So—no more. The sexual revolution is over! England won. No sex! No sex. I'm ready! I'm willing! Let's go!

KEELY AND DU
by Jane Martin

Cole, an abusive alcoholic, 30s
A basement in Rhode Island, the Present
Dramatic

Cole has brutally raped his ex-wife, Keely, who was subsequently kidnapped by a militant anti-abortion group. It is the group's intent to keep Keely a prisoner until the child she carries is at term. In the meantime, they have sought out Cole and cleaned him up in hopes that Keely will forgive him and want to become a family again. Here, the newly "saved" Cole begs Keely for forgiveness.

O   O   O

COLE: Take me back. Forgive me. I loved you in a bad way, a terrible way, and I sinned against your flesh and spirit. God forgive me. I'm an alcoholic but I don't drink now. I don't know . . . I was . . . lived like . . . didn't know right from wrong, but I'm with Jesus now. I accept him as my Lord and he leads me in his path. I will stay on the path. I will stay on the path. We were married, Keely, you are carrying my baby, let's start from there. I put you on a pedestal, Keely, I do, I wouldn't say it, and I am in the mud, I'm drowning and I ask you to lift me up and then we minister to this child. Jeez, Keely, our child. You know in my house, in my father's house, Jeez, what were those kids, they were nuthin', they were disposable. In your house, right, you know what a time you had. You know. But it can be different for him. I'm different, look in my eyes, you know that. Hey, my temper, you know, I don't do that, it's over. (*Indicating Walter.*) Ask him is it over. I think about you every minute, everyday. I want to dedicate my life to you, because it's owed, it's owed to you. You got my baby. I hurt you so bad you would kill a baby! That's not you, who would describe you, you would do that? Jeez, Keely, don't kill the baby. I brought a book we could look up names, we could do that tonight. You pick the name, I would be proud. I'm going to wait on you. You're the boss. They got me a job. I'm employed. Five o'clock, I'm coming home. Boom. No arguments. I help with the house, we can be partners, I understand that guys, you know, we didn't get it, you know, that was yesterday, that's over. I'm back from the dead. I don't say you should believe me but because the baby you should test me out. You gotta take my hand here, we could start from there, I'm asking you. (*His hand extended, he waits, a long time.*) Come on, Keely. I love you. I can't make love to another woman, you know what I mean. (*His hand is still out.*) You loved me and I destroyed that out of the bottle. But, Jeez, look at me, took off 30 pounds, I don't care what they tell me at AA, I'm never taking another drink. I'm never. I wanted to suffer what you suffered so I had them whip me, I wanted to take off the flesh, I wanted more pain. I wanted more pain. I wanted more pain. I wanted your pain. I wanted to be even with you so I could put out my hand and we could be one to one. Come on, take my hand. Come on, Keely. Come on, Keely. (*A time.*) I dream of your body, baby. For all those years I knew the small of your back, it's burned into my hand. I worship your body, I adore you. Come on. Come on. (*He moves off the chair.*) You don't have to ask me to be on my knees, I'm on my knees. What am I without you? I'm only what I did to you. I can't demand. What could I demand? Choose to lift me up. Who else can you save, Keely, but me? I'm the only one you can save. (*His hand is inches from hers.*) Take my hand, come on. It's five inches, you know what I mean? It's right here. It's right here for us to do. We held hands before we kissed. Who can say that? Like it doesn't work that way anymore, right? You don't have to make me promises, I'm not saying that. How could I expect that. I'm saying take the hand alone. (*A short wait.*) Let me touch your hand. Don't speak. Don't speak, I'm saying. Let me come this far and touch your hand, okay? Okay? Just the touch. Okay? You know what people are when they touch you. You got a sixth sense for that. I'm going to touch you, you know, no more than that. No talking. (*He touches her hand. She doesn't withdraw it.*) Oh, my God. Oh, my God, there is stuff leaving me. Okay, Keely, I thought about a pledge, what I could make to you, if I could touch you. No harm. No harm is what I thought of. Look, I want to turn your hand over, make it palm up, okay?

This is make or break, Keely. Right now. Right now. Close your hand, take my hand. You know what I mean? One gesture, you could save me. We could raise a child. With one gesture we could do that. Come on, Keely. Come on, Keely.

LIGHT SENSITIVE
by Jim Geoghan

Lou, a man who has just escaped from Vermont, 30s
An apartment in Hell's kitchen, the Present
Seriocomic

Lou searched for a mate at the New School in Manhattan and believed that he had discovered the perfect woman in Mona, a classmate. They moved to Vermont together with the intention of starting a brand new life together. After a short while, Lou returns to NYC with the following tale of woe.

O   O   O

LOU: Aw . . . I had the Christmas from Hell. You're talkin' to a very depressed and disillusioned person. Mona comes to pick me up and the first thing I realize is she drives a Citroen. You know this car? Lays low to the ground until you start—then the whole thing lifts up like a vacuum cleaner.
[**TOM:** So?]
LOU: So it's the stupidest car ever made. If schmucks had an official car it would be a Citroen. I shoulda known right then. I should never of gotten into that car. We get to Mona's parents' house and the first person I meet is Mona's sister Jane. "Jane has an alternate lifestyle," Mona's tellin' me. "Jane has an alternate lifestyle." I figured that means she's a vegetarian or she hang glides or somethin'. Jane turns out to be a lesbian. I mean a *veteran* lesbian. A confirmed, dedicated, card-carrying, short haircut, khaki pants with heavy-duty work shoes lesbian! And Jane's brought her "friend" Bobby. Actually it's Roberta, but nobody's called her that since Eisenhower was president. Then I meet Mona's father. "He was blacklisted," Mona's been tellin' me. Like it was some honor. Fine, he was blacklisted. I never had the nerve to ask, "Blacklisted from *what*?" I just kept my mouth shut and looked impressed. Mona's mother comes in the room and her folks begin the Christmas Eve "festivities." Her father goes, he goes, "Mona, Jane . . . your mother and I are getting a divorce." Holy mackerel. Did it hit the fan! What went on for the next five hours!

There's no way to describe how tense and nervous and weird and painful everything was. If it had been my family, someone woulda got a gun and killed everyone. At least it woulda been over quick. Not Mona's family. They believe in squeezing out every drop of suffering and agony through *talking*. Mona takes her father into the den, Jane-the-lesbian takes mom in the kitchen. No one comes out for an hour. Mona finally comes out. She wants to talk to mom. Jane talks with papa. Another hour. There's wailin' and cryin'. You hear bits of stuff being said, "She never forgave me!" "His work has been his wife!" "I can't take it anymore." Mona wants to talk with the mother and the father. Jane wants to talk to Mona and mom. I start tryin' to figure out how long it will take to go through all these combinations of people. Mona's ex-husband Bob drops by. All my math is shot to hell! Bob is dropping off their kid. He's twelve. Weird, sick-looking little weasel who takes forty different pills a day for all the stuff that's wrong with 'im. Mona can't wait to spread the joy. "Sweetheart, grandma and grandpa are getting divorced!" The kid goes into an asthma attack like I never seen! People are screamin' an' cryin', "You did this! This is your fault! Call an ambulance! No, don't!" You know, the TV was on through all this. Here these two old farts are ending a marriage of fifty years on Christmas Eve and there's Andy Williams singin' "Holy Night" from Hawaii. Mona's ex hasn't left. He just keeps goin', "Anything I can do?" Finally, Mona takes me aside and says, "Lou, Bob and I are going out for coffee." Then she tells the weasel with asthma, "Honey, sometimes mommies and daddies have coffee even though they're not married." Perfect, now the kid is *completely* messed up. So, Mona and her ex-husband go out for coffee. I spent my Christmas Eve playin' checkers with Bobby-the-lesbo listening to two old communists cry upstairs. We played maybe ten games in a row, didn't speak a word, either one of us. Gets to be one in the mornin', Mona and Bob ain't back yet from havin' their "coffee"—I guess they make *real* good coffee in Vermont—all you can hear is the sound of the clock tickin' and the wind outside. No one's said a word for hours, and all of a sudden Bobby says, "You know, Lou, I'm a lesbian." And I've got to be polite and act *surprised*. Go, Really?" When all I really want to say is, "Oh, I just thought you *liked* looking like Ernest Borgnine!" Or, "Let's go look under the tree. Maybe Santa's left you a Black and Decker vibrator!" That was my Christmas in Vermont I didn't go skiin'. I didn't go tobogganin', or talk with colorful old guys spinnin' yarns. Mona an' me did *not* look for a house to rent or jobs to get. That plan was abandoned instantly. It was just a stupid pipe dream. I was lookin' to make a miracle happen and they don't come that easy.

THE LINE THAT PICKED UP 1000 BABES (AND HOW IT CAN WORK FOR YOU)
by Eric Berlin

Charlie, a man getting drunk in a bar, 20–30
A singles bar
Seriocomic

When Charlie is approached by a woman claiming to know him, he feels compelled to deliver the following diatribe.

O   O   O

CHARLIE: It's a *very* small world. *Very* small. I ran into some girl before, she comes up to me like we're the oldest of friends. Her name's Joan, Jane, John, something like that. You know who she turns out to be? She's my . . . wait, wait, I want to get this straight. She's my ex-girlfriend's sister's friend's *older brother's* ex-girlfriend. Is that stretching it or what? And here I am talking to her like I may have at one time saved her life. "Hi, how you doing, been a long time, yeah." I can't believe I recognized her. What, did I see her *once*, maybe twice. Maybe said five words to her. And two of them were "Gesundheit." And the damn thing is, it happens all the time. Makes me feel like I'm losing my mind sometime. I pass people out on the street, they say hello to me, say hello to them, I walk away saying, who the fuck was that? It gets to the point that I say hello to every person I make eye contact with. I mean, I don't know why I babble when I get drunk, it's just something I do, I babble. My friends say "You babble when you get drunk," and they're right, it's something I do, I babble. Because I don't care too much when it's a guy says hello to me and I don't know who he is. I mean, it bothers me a little, but I'm not going to spend the day agonizing over it. But the girls, I get these pretty girls who are just so happy to see me, and I'm happy to see them too, and I'd be even happier if I knew who they fucking were! But, you know, you can't ask, right? You can't tell some girl you don't know who she is, she'll be insulted. Right? Right?
[**DIANE:** I don't know . . .]
CHARLIE: See, I'll prove it, who the fuck are you?

THE LINE THAT PICKED UP 1000 BABES (AND HOW IT CAN WORK FOR YOU)
by Eric Berlin

Alan, a man trying to pick up a woman in a bar
A singles bar
Seriocomic

When Alan approaches Diane with the intention of getting to know her, her chilly response brings out the worst in him.

O   O   O

ALAN: (*His frustration and anger build gradually as he delivers this.*) I'm a nice guy. I'm a goddamn nice guy. I say that not because *I* think it's true but because that's what everybody says. If you ask any girl who's known me for more than a week, that's how they'll describe me. "Alan? He's a nice guy." They say that because, *you* know, hell, you know nice guys, right? Don't try to hurt people, try to be a gentleman. Treat people right, especially girls. Because that's what we learned girls are attracted to, they want to be treated right. Right? You get a bunch of girls together and get them talking about guys, and they'll dream you up the perfect gentleman. But when it comes to real life, oh man!, that's very different. Because you get those girls together and get them talking about *real* men, not figments of their imagination but *real people,* and what do you get? (*Mimicking.*) "Ohhh, men are scum! Men are slime! Men are *shits!*" (*You* notice how all those words begin with "S"? I think there's something to that.) So men are all these "S" words, all these and more, but who do the girls date? Who comes on to them at the bars and who do they go home with? The *slime*! The *shits*! And then after they get hurt, and they always do, they call me up to confide in me, because long ago we decided that we were "just going to be friends." (I swear, you girls need to get a whole new vocabulary; you girls have started so many goddamn clichés it's not even funny.) So these girls call me up and they say, "Alan, all guys are *sliiiime!*" and then they realize that they're *talking* to a guy, and they say, "Oh, except you, Alan, you're a Nice

54

Guy. When you find a girlfriend, she's going to be such a lucky girl. But it can't be me because, well, I'm attracted to guys that are going to shit all over me." So great. So now I've got all the friends I need, so why should I be a nice guy anymore? Huh? I think I'll be a shit now. Yeah! I think I'll learn some stupid pick-up lines and use them on girls who are dressed to get laid. I think I'll be proud of how loud I can belch. I think I'll use women like they're Black and Decker screwdrivers! Sure! That's what girls really want to hear! So great! Life begins now, okay? *Okay?* Come on, babe, let's go home and *fuck*!

LION IN THE STREETS
by Judith Thompson

Father Hayes, a priest haunted by the past, 60s
A church confessional
Dramatic

When Father Hayes is visited by a man he thought dead, he confesses that he has always felt responsible for his death.

○   ○   ○

FATHER HAYES: I looked at you, David, because . . . I . . . because . . . I wanted . . . to . . . remember . . . you.

[**DAVID:** Remember me?]

FATHER HAYES: Because . . . of what was to happen, in the water: oh *oh* when the day arrived, when the picnic came round, in July, that Canada Day picnic? I had a bad feeling, I had . . . a very bad feeling indeed. We all piled out of the cars: families priests, nuns, altar boys, piled out and lugged all those picnic baskets to tables under trees. The grownups all fussed with food and drink while the kids, all of you children, ran ran in your white bare feet to the water, throwing stones and balls, and a warning sound a terrible, the sound of deep nausea filled my ears and I looked up and saw you, dancing on the water, and I saw a red circle, a red, almost electric circle, dazzling round and round like waves, spinning round your head and body, I thought watch, watch that boy, on this day he will surely drown, he *will*. David, *I knew that you would die.* And all because of the chicken. The twenty-nine-pound chicken brought there by Mrs. Henry grown on her brother's farm, everyone had talked and talked about that chicken, who would carve that chicken, Mrs. Henry took it out you skipped along the shore, she laid it on the table, *"Father Hayes, you go ahead and carve, and don't make a mess of it or you won't see me at mass next Sunday."* Everyone laughed laughed the men, the men drinking beer, watching me sure they're thinking, "Watch him carve like a woman," most men hate priests, you know this is a fact, I could see them thinking cruel thoughts under hooded eyes and practiced grins; my sin was the sin of pride! The sin of pride, David, I started to carve, didn't want to look up lest I wreck the bird. You see at the moment that chicken was worth more, indeed worth more . . . than your *life*, David, *I shut out* the warning voice and I— carved. I carved and carved and ran into trouble, real trouble I remember thinking, "Damn how does any person do it, it's a terrible job," people behave as if it's nothing, but it's terrible, I kept at it, I wouldn't give up, I wouldn't look up till I'd finished, and I finished carving, and I had made a massacre. The men turned away the women . . . murmured comfort, and before I looked up I had a hope, a hard hope, that you were still skipping on the rocks and shouting insults to your pals all hands reached for chicken and bread, potato salad, chocolate cake I looked I looked up and your hand from the sea, your hand, far away, was reaching, reaching for me far away . . . oh no! I ran, and tripped, fell on my face ran again, I could not speak ran to the water and shouted as loud as I could but my voice was so tiny; I saw your hand, ran to the fisherman close, he wasn't home his fat daughter and I, in the skiff, not enough wind no wind, paddling paddling, you a small spot nothing then nothing the sun burns our faces our red red faces.

[**DAVID**: And I . . . was . . . never found?]

FATHER HAYES: And now . . . you have come!! You have finally come!!

LONELY PLANET
by Steven Dietz

Carl, an enigmatic patron of the map shop, 30s
A small map store, the Present
Seriocomic

Carl, a frequent visitor to "Jody's Maps," here denounces the bland nature of human intercourse.

○   ○   ○

CARL: Can I just say this? Can I just say this one thing?

[**JODY**: Certainly.]

CARL: Everyone is boring. How did this happen? *When* did this happen? At some imperceptible moment everyone became absolutely shuffle-your-feet, stare-out-the-window *boring*. I try, okay? I do my part. I strike things up. I toss out words to grease the conversation. But these people at the bus or the market or the newsstand, these people bore me. Not just a little. They bore me a lot. I'm sure they all came from good families, but over time they've lost what small part of them was ever of interest to anyone. They are even sort of hard to *see*.

[**JODY**: Carl?]

[**CARL:** Yes?]

[**JODY**: Where did this chair come from?]

CARL: Two weeks, maybe three—that's all I can stand of anyone, anymore. Then things fall silent. We sit. I hear the beer fill the glass. One of us coughs. "My dentist convinced me to switch from a medium to a soft head." How was your day?" We sit. The waiter takes our glasses. We sit. It's come to this.

[**JODY**: Carl—]

CARL: I know. I've read the books. I can imagine people in their underwear. That helps, for a while. Then their underwear starts to bore me. So, I imagine them without their underwear, and then their embarrassment bores me. So, I imagine them in my underwear and that's moderately exciting until they roll over, drop ashes on my pillow, and say, "I heard this joke at the cash machine today. You're gonna love it. It'll kill you." And they're right. It does. The yawn begins in my groin and stops at their eyes. I watch shadows fill the room like a cancer.

[**JODY**: Carl—]

CARL: So, finally, I try to imagine these people as someone else and soon *that* person bores me, and I imagine that person as someone else and *they* bore me, and so on and so on until I've imagined them all into something so small and distant and insignificant that there is nothing left but me standing alone at the bus stop, alone at the market, alone at the newsstand— reading an article about the tidal wave of boredom that is sweeping the nation. And naturally, the article bores me.

All I'm saying is this: Don't step out your door in the morning until you've thought of something interesting to say.

THE MARRIAGE FOOL
by Richard Vetere

Robert, a man who is afraid of marriage
A home in Queens, the Present
Seriocomic

Robert has fallen in love with Susan but is afraid of what marriage may do to their relationship. Here, he reveals his deepest fears.

O   O   O

ROBERT: . . . But the other side of me says, "Watch out, Rob, watch out." Picture it now. There you are, the two of you sitting in front of the TV, night after night after night . . . just like *they* did. Sometimes you'll sit there for hours never saying a word! And everywhere you go in the house . . . she'll be there . . . doing *things* . . . making noises . . . complaining, dragging you slowly into her life. And you'll be doing the same thing to her! Ruining her vitality, her dreams, with your failures, your mistakes! And sooner or later you will begin to cheat on her! Come on, Rob, when the hell have you ever been faithful? And worse than that, not only will you cheat on her, but you'll resent her for it! You'll have some mad affair in the middle of the afternoon and you'll go home to her and she'll be there, doing what she always does, as if nothing has happened! And you will think to yourself—how can she be so goddamn stupid not to see it? And worse than that, what is the hardest thing to live with, is that you love her! You love every thing about her! Just watching her wake up in the morning gives you a thrill! Being close to her makes you feel warm inside! And it's killing you! All the duplicity, the insecurities, the silences will exhaust you! And after a couple of years you will wonder *who* is she thinking about when she gets that faraway look in her eyes! What louse of a creep in her past still stirs memories? Or, maybe, she's having an affair? Some low life, like yourself, has come along at the right time and with romance and lies, just like the ones you use, has got her attention! He's got her lonely, drifting body and soul for a few hours once every two weeks and she'll come home and see you there doing whatever you do, and she'll think to herself, how can he be so damn stupid not to see what I'm doing? And she'll resent you like you resent her and in the end the marriage will have nothing to do with caring at all but *enduring*. Seeing who will outlive who. Standing by their grave when it is all over. *Crying your heart out*. Realizing then how much you really love them, want them, need them, and you never saw it! (*Pause.*) I never want to get married. Never! Ever! I fear it worse than death itself! I despise it!

THE MIDNIGHT MOONLIGHT
WEDDING CHAPEL
by Eric Berlin

Walter, a man witnessing a wedding, 30s
A wedding chapel in Las Vegas
Seriocomic

When a couple whose marriage he has witnessed decides to file for divorce, Walter lectures them on the importance of making a commitment.

○   ○   ○

WALTER: What I want to tell you is this: I saw on Donahue last week these five couples all of whom stay together despite the fact that the guy knocks the shit out of the woman on a daily basis. The women were there on stage, too, toothless wonders all of them. They stayed with these guys because they know deep down that the men really love them. And besides, they didn't get hit unless they did something *really* wrong. Like *breathe* wrong, or *I* don't know, drop *a plate* or something. And you know what? You know *what?* I'm beginning to think *they're* sane and that *you* people are the crazies. You've *got* to be crazy! Here these people are battling it out on a daily basis and you don't want to marry her because she makes things out of *wire??* *Deal with it!* This is such a drawback? This is enough to make you say, "No"? "There's a more perfect woman out there, just like her except she doesn't use wire as a medium. In a perfect world, my wife uses—" What? Pastels? In *this* world? In *today's* world you're shooting for perfection. No. Sorr-ree, pal, it's not going to happen. Because you'll find something wrong with the perfect match, too. Because to accept someone for good is to admit out loud that you are not strong enough to handle things alone, that you need someone to accompany you. And what is wrong with this? *Nothing* is. I think it happens every day. But we get scared and we say, "*I* can be alone, *I* am just as happy then as now." We lie to ourselves all the time. You guys have something everybody wants, my dumb-ass friend there, everyone I know. Me. Everybody on the goddamn planet wants what you have and you're backing off from it out of fear. And don't give me these excuses about other people because it's fear, I know. If you *think* you're happy, you probably are, don't shoot for the moon. I mean, I mean—You wanna dump this guy because of a *police scanner*. (And, my brother has a police scanner, it's the most annoying device in this galaxy, squawking like that, *but do I disown my brother*? Go out and get a dog instead? *No!*) What kind of . . . do you see what I'm—. . . *Stay* with each other. If it wasn't going to work, you would have known in the course of the goddamn quarter-century you've already *spent* with each other. (*Pause. Wired.*) Have I made myself *clear*??

NORTHEAST LOCAL
by Tom Donaghy

Mickey, a man facing a midlife crisis, 40s
The home of Mickey and Gi
Dramatic

Years of drinking and a failed career have taken their toll on Mickey, who announces at Thanksgiving dinner that he is leaving his wife.

○   ○   ○

MICKEY: So, yeah, anyway, we're talking, hoisting a few . . . elbows—speculating on how Kelly, with or without his belly, cause Kelly ain't a looker himself with or without it, right? We're speculating on how he nabbed this one with the hair, the—the whole look. So Hughie Walsh—mouth on this guy—Walshie just screams it out, goes, loud as all—goes, "Hey, Kelly! aren't you dating over your head on the food chain?" Oh, and Kelly goes beat red, purple, blue, turns every color in the coloring book cause it turns out, this chick's his sister. And her name's Shelly!
   [**MAIR**: Shelly Kelly.]
MICKEY: The name's Shelly Kelly!
   [**MAIR**: Just said it!]
MICKEY: It's his goddamn sister!
   [**GI**: Mick, Mair don't like the language—]
   [**MAIR**: Dark meat, please.]
MICKEY: Oh, we had a laugh out of that, let me tell ya—
   [**GI**: Where's Stefan?]
MICKEY: And she's so—and Kelly's pretty ugly, pretty hard to face except without a few in you, which we had, did I mention it?
   [**JESSE**: Once or twice, Mick.]
MICKEY: And we're all talking, she's a nice gal, Shelly. She's interested what everyone's doing, ok, me and her get to shooting the—
   [**MAIR**: Dark meat!]
MICKEY: —get to talking. She's going on, alls she ever wanted, meet the right guy and all, ok? But they're all just interested in

her—they like her hair, how she dresses what not. So—buy her a drink, Mickey, I'm thinking. Well, ladies drink free on Thursday but I pretend to buy her one, ok. Cause she seems like she needs someone to pretend just a bit, so I do it. We talk some more, yu-ta-da. Haven't talked to anyone new—all the same old faces. So it's good to talk to a new person everyone once in a—told her about Gi, the boy. Pictures in my wallet. And Kelly's asleep in his beer for, you know, an hour at this point, so I volunteer to take her home.

[**MAIR**: No one's passing the wings.]

MICKEY: Walk her to her door.

[**JESSE**: Mick.]

MICKEY: (*Pause.*) So Shelly thought this was sweet. Nothing for me. But felt sweet. I felt sweet. Haven't felt sweet . . . in years. And I go in her place, real sweet for a single girl and there we are so I go . . . go . . . "Who do I have to kiss to get a drink around here?"

[**GI**: Won't come down.]

MICKEY: And she smiled. (*Pause.*) Haven't seen a smile like that in . . . don't know how long. (*Pause.*) So I kissed her. (*Pause.*) But she didn't back. We seemed to be getting on and all but guess cause . . . cause I told her about Gi, the boy.

[**GI**: . . . Stefan.]

MICKEY: *Know* his name. And how I can't keep a job for my family to have anything. And how Gi likes nice stuff. How I drink away the little we got, how I owe everyone, and no one wants a welder, cause a machines, how we just had the one kid cause a . . . some reason or other. You know, I love kids. Feel like one myself, told her. And kissed her a little more. Told her everything while I kissed her little. (*Pause.*) Gonna go to bed now. And in the morning guess I'll be moving away. Like I mentioned probably be best thing for everyone involved. Did I mention that? Probably once or twice.

ON THE OPEN ROAD
by Steve Tesich

Angel, a scavenger, 20–30
A bombed-out museum in a country experiencing a civil war
Seriocomic

As Angel and his partner loot a museum that has been destroyed by war, he tells the story of how the conflict began.

O　　　O　　　O

ANGEL: If I was God, I'd change some things in the Bible. About how you shouldn't make graven images of God. If I was God, I wouldn't give a shit if they made graven images of me. What do I care? I'm God. Can't hurt me to be graven. Nothing can hurt me. I'm God. But I would put in its place, in big letters: Thou shalt not make graven images of your fellow man. (*He pauses to rest a bit.*) The very first time I ever went to a museum was right before the Civil War broke out. (*Continues to work.*) It was one of those scum-of-the-earth days at the museum. If you're scum, you get in free. These social agencies rounded us up and took us there in school buses. About three hundred of us. Young scum. Old scum. Half-way house scum. No-house scum. A cross-section. It was in order to uplift us they took us there. I was delighted to be in that air-conditioned place. That by itself was uplifting enough for me. (*The statue is now high enough. Al moves the cart under it. Angel lowers it slowly, as Al guides it.*) But there was this exhibit there in the museum. These artworks of a contemporary nature. And every work of art showed some man or woman or kid who was having a real bad time of it. Street-type sufferers and the like. We're snickering among ourselves in that stupid scum-of-the-earth way of ours. What? We came all the way here to see more scum like us. But the others, the regular people, in chic lightweight summer suits and dresses with brochures in their hands, they're not snickering at all. And they're offended 'cause we are. They are seriously moved by what they see in the exhibit. They are telling each other how beautiful it all is, this exhibit of human suffering. I try to ignore them, but was like the air-conditioning broke down or something, 'cause I start feeling hot. It's rubbing me all wrong to hear about the beauty of it all. Not far from the museum, twenty blocks or so uptown where I lived, there was the same kind of exhibit. Same kind of suffering. Only it wasn't beautiful there. And there were no couples in chic lightweight summer clothes to be moved by it all. What was fucking scum-of-the earth outside the museum was a fucking masterpiece inside. And then this thing starts crawling through my brain. This really painful idea that maybe there was something in me worth seeing, that nobody would ever see so long as these artworks were there. I know what I'm thinking, but I'm trying not to think it, 'cause it's no good thinking such thoughts. But then I hear it. It's like I hear the other scum-of-the-earth there thinking the same thing. And suddenly it's a much bigger thought. It's like ants. I read in this nature magazine once that ants don't have brains and that ants don't talk unless there's enough of them that get together. Two ants got nothing to say to each other. They don't know what to do. But if a few hundred of them get together, a brain is born. Suddenly, we started trashing it all. Breaking up statues and tearing paintings to shreds. There were these armed guards there and they shot a bunch of us, but we didn't care. Ants don't really care if a bunch gets killed. We set fire to the museum and ran out into the street. (*The cart is loaded. The tarp is over the cart. The ladder now hangs from some pegs on its side.*)

[**AL:** And so another Civil War began.]

ANGEL: For once I was there at the start of something. It was very pleasant to realize you didn't really have to be highly qualified to make history.

PLAY WITH REPEATS
by Martin Crimp

Tony, a man living parts of his life over again, 20–30
A city, the Present
Dramatic

Tony has been given the gift of living parts of his life over again but soon finds himself trapped in a repeating loop. Here, he reencounters a couple in a pub for the second time.

○   ○   ○

TONY: No, I see what this must look like, but it isn't what you think. I mean I'm not making a play for you or anything. I'm aware that you have commitments and I respect that. If I'm drawn to you—and I am—it's because I'm drawn to you as a couple. You make a very attractive couple. (*As if she were about to speak.*) No, please, I think these things should be said.

I've always thought: I know her from somewhere, we've met. We've spoken before. But now I see that what it is is you're very like somebody. You've heard that before. Of course. But you genuinely are. You're genuinely like Franky where I work. Which is short for Frances. By which I don't mean to belittle you. Because of course you're unique. We're all of us unique. I'm just talking about a resemblance.

Perhaps I'm intruding—and if I am forgive me—but I've been doing a lot of thinking this evening. I've been sitting over there. You've probably noticed me. It's where I normally sit. I've been thinking about the past, and watching you both, and I find myself drawn.

I've been trying to think of my earliest memory. What's your earliest memory? I think mine is wearing red plastic sandals. It's summer and I'm wearing red plastic sandals. I'm looking at the sky and I notice that it's full of little bright specks, like sparks. I asked my teacher: what are the little bright specks I see? She told me: those are germs.

Do you think she really believed they were germs? (*Faint smile from Kate, who looks at him for the first time.*) And if not, what was she trying to do to me? I'd like to ask her that.

You see I've been watching you both. Not in that sense. No if I wanted to watch that—which I don't—I could go and pay for it. But I've been watching you both, and what I observe is that you don't talk to each other.

Which perhaps means that you don't need to—which is all very well—it's all very well, but it makes me curious. And stop me, please stop if you feel I'm intruding but it makes me curious as to what you really feel.

You don't talk. Now maybe that's love. I'd like to think so. But maybe there's something else. Something that eats away at you inside. That's all. I only ask because I'm curious as to what you really feel. Perhaps it eats away at you. And maybe if you talked. . . .

Because you're welcome to come back. Both of you are welcome to come back with me and talk. It's a small place, but if you don't mind sitting on the bed. . . . (*Nick has joined them.*)

[**NICK:** Excuse me.]

TONY: This isn't what you think.

SERPENT IN THE NIGHT SKY
by Dianne Warren

Preacher, an enigmatic minister, 40s
A small town stretching along the shore of an immense lake in
Northern Saskatchewan, the Present
Dramatic

*Here, Preacher recounts a hallucinatory experience to a friend
who has heard this story many times before.*

O   O   O

PREACHER: I want to tell you a story, Stella.

[**STELLA:** If it's the one about the Cambodians, I've heard it.]

PREACHER: It was long time ago now. Almost twenty years.

[**STELLA:** Preacher. I've heard this story.]

PREACHER: November. Maybe December.

[**STELLA:** There was snow on the ground.]

[**PREACHER:** That's right, Stella. Yeah.]

[**STELLA:** See. I've heard it.]

PREACHER: I had crossed the Canadian border, wheeled my bike across in the dark.

[**STELLA:** Preacher . . . (*Resigning herself.*)]

PREACHER: Everybody said you should steer clear of the big east and west coast crossings so I picked Montana. I crossed at Willow Creek, just north of Havre. Nothing to it. It was maybe 6 o'clock in the morning. Still dark, but there was a big moon. And damned if I didn't see an eclipse. I pulled my bike over on the side of the road and watched. It was half an hour, may forty minutes before the moon was right again. I was watching it, you know, and I was thinking . . . it was weird, the way it got so dark . . . I was thinking this snake had swallowed the moon . . . You see pictures of them sometimes with these giant bulges in their guts. Have you seen them, Stella? Those pictures? (*Stella is standing so her pregnant belly is visible.*)

[**STELLA:** Yeah. I've seen them.]

PREACHER: Anyway, this snake had swallowed the moon and the nights were never going to be light again. It was sad. (*Pause.*) I cried. I did. I actually cried. I sat by the side of the road, the first night of the rest of my life, and cried. I cried, Stella.

[**STELLA:** I know.]

PREACHER: I never forgot that snake. (*Pause.*) There was lots of stuff about east Asia in the papers back then . . . and I read one day that these Cambodian soldiers had injured fifty of their own people by shooting at the moon. Turns out they were trying to keep the moon from being eaten by a giant snake. Everybody thought they were nuts. That's why it was in the paper. (*Pause.*) I've always remembered that snake. You see, Stella, I don't have time for weddings.

SNAKEBIT
by David Marshall Grant

Jonathan, a self-centered actor, 30–40
A house in LA, the Present
Dramatic

Jonathan has just discovered that his wife slept with his best friend, Michael, just before they were married. Michael, who is gay, has just tested positive for HIV, and Jonathan here confronts his friend with his own feelings of fear and loss.

O   O   O

JONATHAN: I can't believe you never told me you slept with my wife three months before I was married. Don't say anything. I don't want you to say anything. I just think there's been too many secrets at the table, that's all. I don't want any more secrets, okay. I'm out in the hallway, you're in the kitchen. God, I miss you Michael. I want us to be closer. I need you, really. Please. I'm going to a shrink, okay? I'm going to cure myself. I have to. Nobody likes me anymore. She'll come home, I know she will. I mean, we've been married ten years, you make allowances. I'm a shit I admit it. But what nobody seems to give me credit for, is I hate myself. I accomplish a thing just to see how worthless it is. I know that. I eat myself basically. I keep winning, watching it prove nothing but my own failure. She's the only thing I didn't win, Michael. She took me. I don't know why. I have to keep her. We'll make up. We've been doing it for a decade. And if we can't, we'll bury it, like nuclear waste, and we'll move on. We've done it before. That's what people do. Do you remember when your mother died and I hugged you? I was a better person then. I want to help you. I'm sorry, I don't know what to say. You gotta feel snakebit. Michael, you're going to be fine. They know so much more now. I know you're going to be fine.

SOMEONE WHO'LL WATCH OVER ME
by Frank McGuiness

Adam, an American held hostage, 30–40
A cell, the Present
Seriocomic

Adam shares a cell in Lebanon with Michael and Edward who both hail from the British Isles. Here, Adam laments his lack of American underwear.

O   O   O

ADAM: I want a pair of jockey shorts. I want to wear my country's greatest contribution to mankind. Fresh, white jockey shorts. A man's underwear. That's why Arabs can't wear them. If their shorts don't have hole in them, they can't find their dicks. I want a pair of jockey shorts. I want to kill an Arab. Just one. Throw his body down before his mother and father, his wife and kids, and say, I did it, me, the American. Now you can blame me. You are justified in what you do to me. You have deserved this. I want to see their faces fill with hate. True hate. I want that within my power.

SOMEONE WHO'LL WATCH OVER ME
by Frank McGuiness

Michael, a British subject held hostage in Lebanon, 40s
A cell, the Present
Seriocomic

*Michael and his fellow hostage, Edward, celebrate Christmas in
their dismal cell in Lebanon. Here, Michael tells how he lost his
wife.*

O   O   O

MICHAEL: A car crash. She was driving to work. It was the month
of May. I wasn't with her. I was revising an article at home. I
answered the phone and the university told me she was un-
conscious, at the scene of the accident. I knew. I sat by the
phone. Half an hour later they rang to say she was dead. I
went to identify her. She looked like a child who'd fallen off
her bike. It was me persuaded her to buy a car. We were both
working. We could afford a car. Full of love and goodness.
Gone. Such is life. I slept for some time afterwards with the
bedroom light on. Then one night I switched off the light.
Gone. Happy Christmas, Edward.

SPINNING INTO BLUE
by Sally Nemeth

Atkinson, an ornithologist for the State Wildlife Commission, 30s
A river property on the Tennessee-Tombigbee Waterway, the
Present.
Dramatic

*In this isolated moment, Atkinson speaks of the necessity of let-
ting go in order to find ecstasy.*

○   ○   ○

ATKINSON: In the dictionary the word "raptor" appears above
the word "rapture." A raptor is defined as either a ravisher,
plunderer or robber, or as an order of birds of prey. Rapture is
described as the act of seizing and carrying off as prey or plun-
der; the act of carrying or state of being carried onwards; the
act of carrying off a woman and the act of conveying a person
from one place to another—especially to heaven. It is also described as the transport of mind; ecstasy. Both words imply
force of movement, and, in either case, there is an active and
passive assignment of roles. The prey, the woman, or the
booty is carried off by the plunderer. The exception to this is
the definition as transport of mind; ecstasy. I believe that's
something one can only do oneself. And it can only be done
by giving up, exerting no force. A leap of faith. This sounds
like the most passive thing a person can do, but I believe it
takes all the will in the world. It is against human nature to let
go, to surrender. We equate it with loss of control; a precious
thing we're warned never to lose. But for that loss, that giving
up, we gain everything and become enraptured, ecstatic. We
can even fly.

STANTON'S GARAGE
by Joan Ackerman

Ron, a man who hasn't gotten over his divorce, 40
A small service station in upstate Missouri, the Present
Dramatic

*On the day of his ex-wife's marriage, Ron tells a fellow traveler
of his sorrow.*

O   O   O

RON: Such an unattractive sound—ex, especially for someone soft
you've held naked against your body at night for a decade.
Like ax.
[**LEE:** How long have you been divorced?]
[**RON:** Five years.]
[**LEE:** That's a long time. That's how long ago my husband
died.]
RON: See, the problem was I never made it to court. For my divorce: I never went. I didn't want to go, I didn't have to go,
my lawyer told me, but. . . it was a mistake. You have to go to
events like that. You have to be there. You have to be at your
. . . birth. To get the full effect. You have to go to funerals,
watch the body being lowered into the ground, being covered
with dirt, shovelful by shovelful. Then you know. . . you know
where the body is. In the ground. There's no doubt. You have
to go to your own divorce, sit in the courtroom, hold your
coat in your lap, look at the judge, look at your lawyer, look at
her lawyer. Make the appropriate expressions. Hear the flies.
Then you have something. Then you have pieces, concrete
pieces. I can't see it. I don't have her face getting divorced. I
never saw our marriage officially pronounced dead. It's been a
problem.

STRANGERS ON EARTH
by Mark O'Donnell

Mutt, a secretly smart carpenter from South Boston, 35
Here and now
Seriocomic

Here, Mutt enjoys a game of garage poker with his buddies.

O   O   O

MUTT: "Here we go, Southie, here we go!" . . . Hey Shemp! Look alive! I got some typically bad news for you! (*He lays down his and triumphantly.*) Snicker snicker sneer sneer! Poor, and I do mean poor, you! (*He rakes in the pot.*) I hate to see dumb animals suffer—Why don't you leave the room? (*He grins in the other direction, to his other brother.*) At least Packy knew enough to fold. He's a very mature thirty-eight. (*Gloats over his winnings.*) —Shemp, you know why they put this little eye in the pyramid on the dollar bill? The little floating radioactive eyeball in the pyramid penthouse? I didn't think you did! It's a hypnotic eye. Sure! You didn't know that? That's what keeps us all in line, the hypnotic eye on the dollar bill. You look at it when you're buying a Hershey bar and it says: "You—love— the—American—way! You—love—the—American—way!" Sure! George Washington's state hypnotist dreamed it up. The mystic master Money. You didn't know that? And the more dollar bills you handle, the more American you get. . . . Well, yeah, quarters do the trick for you, cretins are fascinated by shiny objects! But that's why radicals don't believe. They don't get enough exposure to the hypnotic eye. It all has something to do with Masons, and I don't mean bricklayers! . . .

No thanks, I got a construction job in New York, for the Fairburns. Piece of cake, cheesecake—two Radcliffe broads. You'll have to repossess the Monte Carlo without me. Sorry! (*He deals a new hand. He notices some children have approached the garage where the game is being played. They are unseen by us, as are his brothers.*)

Hey, you kids! This is a private garage! Now get out of here—or I'll saw you into pepper steak! (*He brandishes a*

handy saw, and laughs with pleasure as the children presumably flee squealing.)
    Ha! They love it!

THE TRANSFORMATIONS ON THE BEACH:
A SEXUAL NOH DRAMA
by Dick Bonker

A Traveling Penitent, 30–50
A beach
Dramatic

*Here, a traveling penitent tells the tragic tale of a woman who
lost both her father and her lover on the same day*

O   O   O

TRAVELING PENITENT: She seeks her father and her lover
Who both on the self same day, died
Within an hour of the sun's rising
The old gent began to crumble
He called to her for comfort in his last hour
But when she took his hand
It pulled right off in hers!
He didn't feel the pain
For that, too, began to crumble
His broke off in lumps
"I . . . Had to . . . Merciless . . . Bright"
Then they too were gone
'Desiccated' is the word
The one remaining eye pleaded with her two
Then filled with tears
Which turned to dribblings of dry salt
She tried to kiss his lips
But found them pasty and unfeeling
His nose was sand. Beetles
Scurried through his cheekbones
His once red hair dried up like leaves
It was his October, so to speak
Soon there was little left than a pattern in the sand
Ripples left by long departed waves.

UNFINISHED STORIES
by Sybille Pearson

Walter, a German-born Jew who escaped the Nazis, 80
An apartment on Upper West Side, NYC, the Present
Dramatic

At the end of his life, Walter wishes to die with dignity at the time of his choosing. Here, he gives his grandson the responsibility of making sure that no heroic measures are taken to save him should his attempt at suicide fail.

○   ○   ○

WALTER: You see, my boy, in hospitals, on the many benches, sit the estranged . . . fathers, sons, mothers, husbands . . . incapable of allowing each other to die. "Let him see me once more. Let him open his eyes once more." This they say to their doctor, to me. In that "once more," love will be shown, finally exchanged. I am to put a tube in him. One here. One here. Keep him for me. You understand. Nanu. Which agony? You are the doctor. Which agony do you treat? Your patient's? Who need to die, to be released from this pain. Or the agony of the man or the woman who's waited for love too long? The patient didn't leave a statement with his wishes.
[**DANIEL:** I don't know.]
WALTER: You are responsible. You have to have an answer.
[**DANIEL:** The family.]
WALTER: Nanu. Now, we are a different story. I have no wish to live. I will not see the end of this disease. I know how it ends. I have seen it too often. I tell you this. I have a statement here that needs a witness. You say you will be it. You sign. I ask you not to ask me more questions. I ask you to play chess. You do. (*He turns board so the white pieces face him.*) We play a game of chess. We say good night. I go to my room. I've had brandy. I inject morphine. Perhaps in the morning, I still breathe. Gaby finds me. She cannot let me die as I wish. She cannot be without hope. Nanu. In the hospital, you show the doctor my note. "Yes," he'll say, "but what happened that day?" You will tell him a family argument in the after-

noon. That I asked if Yves called. That he didn't. He is a romantic this doctor. Decides that was the reason I took morphine. There are people like this. He will tell you of a machine that will give me what he calls the gift of time, enough time, he tells you, so I might see this new child. And will you think, "There will be a new grandchild, a good one, the better one. I will be the one to take that from Opa?" That test will be harder than what we do here. (*He holds paper out to Daniel*.) I am dependent on you. Dependent on my evaluation of you.

THE VIEW FROM HERE
by Margaret Dulaney

Arnold, a man whose wife has recently left him, 30s
A home in suburban Kentucky, the Present
Seriocomic

Maple and Stan have been trying to have a baby for 12 years. They've tried just about everything—including wearing wigs to look like different people in bed. Here, a neighbor muses about their plight as it pertains to his own.

O   O   O

ARNOLD: Fellow gets married, wants a baby. Not too much to ask for, just a little baby to love, so he tries a while, prays a little, tries some more, prays harder, tries again, prays with a vengeance, tries one more time and gives up praying. Twelve years and all he gets is a big dial tone in the sky. Figures the Man Upstairs must have fallen asleep, changed neighborhoods, got the stereo cranked too high, so he dreams up something to get His attention. After twelve years of being overlooked, he figures he'd better come up with a humdinger. Eye opener. Things get a little out of hand, and next thing you know, the police pick him up driving around in his wife's Oldsmobile, wearing somebody else's hair. Bernice's hair. . . . Heck, we've all been there, one time or another. Some of us don't leave our houses for six years, figure that'll get His attention. Knew someone finished off a whole jar of mayonnaise, dipping pickles. Then there's the type that set up camp out on the back nine, trying to get a birdie on the 18th. You gotta give Stan credit, I believe if I were looking out from on high, and saw a fellow driving around in somebody else's blond bouffant hairdo, I'd stick around long enough to hear him out. That's all any of us really wants, isn't it? . . . Isn't it Fern? (*He waits for her to look at him.*) Somebody to stick around long enough to hear us out.

WHAT A MAN WEIGHS
by Sherry Kramer

Haseltine, a charmer, 40s
Here and now
Dramatic

After seducing many many women, Haseltine confesses his desire for something that will remain once his lust has been sated.

O   O   O

HASELTINE: All this light. (*He takes the book from her again.*) Did you know that a page in this book is like your skin? (*He touches her cheek, just for an instant.*) Not as soft, maybe, but it ages just as fast, in sunlight. A piece of paper ages a month in an hour in the sun.

[**THE DEBBIE:** It does?]

HASELTINE: Most people don't know it, but it does. Come on. I'll show you that room (*She picks up her books and they go down the steps together. The Debbie goes offstage and Haseltine returns to Joan.*) And I take her to that room. And I leave her. But she comes back. And each time she does, she changes, faster and faster. She runs into me, by accident, in the parking lot. In the front room. By the stairs. She looks up at me—and she's not afraid. She's beautiful. So goddamn beautiful. And then—I can't help it. I have to—have that, don't I? I have to—she's so beautiful, I have to take some of that back, don't I? It's mine, I gave it to her, I have to. . . .

If I could just stop—there—before I have to—touch it, take it back—if I could just freeze it, preserve it, just there, with her looking up from the book she's pretending to read, or that moment she sees me when she's coming down the stairs—if I could stop there, with the secret thing inside her welling up and shining out of her. But I can't. And then—then, afterwards, she wants something else. That's her price, to be so beautiful, to let me see how beautiful she is. She wants something else, and I can't give her that. So punishes me. She isn't beautiful anymore. She won't let that thing in her out. She doesn't understand—she doesn't know how to

83

make it stay. Here I've given her what she needed to be so beautiful, to be so goddamn beautiful, that's the important thing, but no, that doesn't matter, she wants something else. She looks at me, and she isn't beautiful anymore, and she can't understand. Why I can't stay. You understand, Joan?

[**JOAN:** (*A whisper.*) Yes.]

HASELTINE: You're sure? You're sure you want to do this?

[**JOAN:** Yes.]

HASELTINE: You think you can remember—you think you can hold on to it, after—do you think you can make it stay? Because I've been watching you hide it from me for three years now. I've seen it, in that instant when you look up from your work, in the moment you see me when you're coming down the stairs. I've seen how hard you've worked to keep it hidden from me.

Can you work that hard the other way?

WHAT WE DO WITH IT
by Bruce MacDonald

John, a man confronted by his past, 50–60
Here and now
Dramatic

John abused his daughter when she was a little girl. Now she confronts him as an adult, and he is incapable of anything save denial.

O   O   O

JOHN: (*Beat.*) It's easy to believe her, she makes you want to believe her. (*Forces a pathetic laugh.*) *I* want to believe her. But what we are witnessing is the result of . . . I don't know. Sickness. Some kind of sickness, I'm not the expert. She is so, she has so much anger, and the question is, what caused that anger? What caused her to turn against her father with horrible, *horrible* lies. Turned against both her parents, really, because I hate to say this (*To her.*) but it shortened your mother's life, Cheryl. Returning those presents, not coming to the hospital. (*Beat.*) Do I know that for a fact? Of course not. I *feel* it. It took away her will to live. And she never said, Where's Cheryl? Where is my daughter? Not once. And I have to resent that, I do resent it. But she kept her dignity. I don't believe you intended it, I don't think you understood the impact your actions would have. As your mother said, She knows not what she does. I don't mean to be accusing you of something, but you pushed me, Cheryl, you have made me talk about *what really happened.* (*Beat.*) Because if the truth were known, I would have preferred to not speak. I would have preferred to not see you than to see you like this. Sometimes it is a question of decency.

THE YEARS
by Cindy Lou Johnson

Andrew, a young photographer, 30s
Here and now
Dramatic

*On the day of his cousin's wedding, Andrew tells her of his need
to capture life's moments on film.*

O   O   O

ANDREW: People just . . . *kill* me.

    [**ELOISE:** What do you mean.]

ANDREW: I mean we're all so limited. I don't mean financially or
emotionally—I just mean—by life, like somehow our resources
have been severely limited, like we have no maps, no real
guideposts, and in spite of it we seem to want to go on. We
go to sleep and get up and eat these little meals, you know?
And on top of it, someone like Isabella even puts a little flower
by our plates, just for beauty, just for something special, just
so that moment matters. And it kills me. It just practically
breaks me in two. And that's why I have to take these pictures. I have to, just to say to whoever it is, I see you, which—
all right—what does anyone care if I see them, except *I* care. I
mean it *affects* me. I mean when I get right down to it, it's the
main thing that matters to me. I guess my camera is that special thing for me, the little flower I can put by someone's
plate—just a way to say this moment matters.

tended, dates of production, your seating capacity and admission fee. Royalties are payable one week before the opening performance of the play to Samuel French, Inc., at 45 W. 25th Street, New York, NY 10010-2751; or at 7623 Sunset Blvd., Hollywood, CA 90046-2795, or to Samuel French (Canada), Ltd., 80 Richmond Street East, Toronto, Ontario, Canada M5C 1P1.

Royalty of the required amount must be paid whether the play is presented for charity or gain and whether or not admission is charged.

Stock royalty quoted on application to Samuel French, Inc.

45 West 25th St, New York, NY 10010.

LIGHT SENSITIVE by Jim Geoghan. © Copyright, 1992, 1993, by Jim Geoghan. Reprinted by permission of Writers and Artists Agency. For information: William Craver, Writers and Artists Agency, 19 W. 44th St., Suite 1000, New York, NY 10036.

THE LINE THAT PICKED UP 1000 BABES [from BABES AND BRIDES] by Eric Berlin. © Copyright, 1993, by Eric Berlin. Permission to reprint granted by Author and Samuel French Inc., CAUTION: Professionals and amateurs are hereby warned that THE LINE THAT PICKED UP 1000 BABES is subject to a royalty. It is fully protected under the copyright laws of the United States of America, the British Commonwealth, including Canada, and all other countries of the Copyright Union. All rights, including professional, amateur, motion picture, recitation, lecturing, public reading, radio broadcasting, television, and the rights of translation into foreign languages are strictly reserved. In its present form the play is dedicated the reading public only.

The amateur live stage performance rights to THE LINE THAT PICKED UP 1000 BABES are controlled exclusively by Samuel French, Inc., and royalty arrangements and licenses must be secured well in advance of presentation. PLEASE NOTE that amateur royalty fees are set upon publication in accordance with your producing circumstances. When applying for a royalty quotation and license please give us the number of performances intended, dates of production, your seating capacity and admission fee. Royalties are payable one week before the opening performance of the play to Samuel French, Inc., at 45 W. 25th Street, New York, NY 10010-2751; or at 7623 Sunset Blvd., Hollywood, CA 90046-2795, or to Samuel French (Canada), Ltd., 80 Richmond Street East, Toronto, Ontario, Canada M5C 1P1.

Royalty of the required amount must be paid whether the play is presented for charity or gain and whether or not admission is charged.

Stock royalty quoted on application to Samuel French, Inc.

45 West 25th St., New York, NY 10010.

LION IN THE STREETS by Judith Thompson. © Copyright, 1993, BY Judith Thompson. Reprinted by permission of the Author. For information: Great North Artists Management, Inc., 350 Dupont St., Toronto, M5R IV9 Canada.

LONELY PLANET by Steven Dietz. © Copyright, 1993, by Steven Dietz. Reprinted by permission of the Author and ICM, Inc. For information: Brad Kalos, ICM Inc.,40 West 57th Street, New York, NY 10019.

THE MARRIAGE FOOL by Richard Vetere. © Copyright, 1993, by Richard Vetere. Reprinted by permission of Richard Vetere. For information: Mary Meagher, William Morris Agency, 1350 Avenue of the Americas, New York, NY 10019.

THE MIDNIGHT MOONLIGHT WEDDING CHAPEL [from BABES AND BRIDES] by Eric Berlin. © Copyright, 1993, by Eric Berlin. Permission to reprint granted by Author and Samuel French Inc. CAUTION: Professionals and amateurs are hereby warned that THE MIDNIGHT MOONLIGHT WEDDING CHAPEL s subject to a royalty. It is fully protected under the copyright laws of the United States of America, the British Commonwealth, including Canada, and all other countries of the Copyright Union. All rights, including professional, amateur, motion picture, recitation, lecturing, public reading, radio broadcasting, television, and the rights of translation into foreign